Ethnicity and Culture
amidst New "Neighbors"

CULTURAL SURVIVAL STUDIES IN ETHNICITY AND CHANGE

Allyn & Bacon

Series Editors, David Maybury-Lewis and Theodore Macdonald, Jr.
Cultural Survival, Inc., Harvard University

Ethnicity and Culture amidst New "Neighbors":
The Runa of Ecuador's Amazon Region

Theodore Macdonald, Jr.
Harvard University

Allyn and Bacon
Boston • London • Toronto • Sydney • Tokyo • Singapore

Series Editor: Sarah L. Kelbaugh
Editor-in-Chief, Social Science: Karen Hanson
Series Editorial Assistant: Heather Ahlstrom
Executive Marketing Manager: Suzy Spivey
Consulting Editor: Sylvia Shepard
Manufacturing Buyer: Dave Repetto
Cover Designer: Brian Gogolin
Editorial-Production Service: Omegatype Typography, Inc.

ISBN: 0-205-19821-X

Printed in the United States of America
10 9 8 7 6 5 4 3 2 1   03 02 01 00 99 98

All photographs are credited to Theodore Macdonald, Jr.

To my Dad, in Memory

Contents

Foreword to the Series

Cultural Survival is an organization founded in 1972 to defend human rights of indigenous peoples, who are those, like the Indians of the Americas, who have been dominated and marginalized by peoples different from themselves. Since the states that claim jurisdiction over indigenous peoples consider them aliens and inferiors, they are among the world's most underprivileged minorities, facing a constant threat of physical extermination and cultural annihilation. This is no small matter, for indigenous peoples make up approximately five percent of the world's population. Most of them wish to become successful ethnic minorities, meaning that they be permitted to maintain their own traditions even though they are out of the mainstream in the countries where they live. Indigenous peoples hope, therefore, for multi-ethnic states that will tolerate diversity in their midst. In this their cause is the cause of ethnic minorities worldwide and is one of the major issues of our times, for the vast majority of states in the world are multi-ethnic. The question is whether states are able to recognize and live peaceably with ethnic differences, or whether they will treat them as an endless source of conflict.

Cultural Survival works to promote multi-ethnic solutions to otherwise conflictive situations. It sponsors research, advocacy, and publications that examine situations of ethnic conflict, especially (but not exclusively) as they affect indigenous peoples, and suggests solutions for them. It also provides technical and legal assistance to indigenous peoples and organizations.

This series of monographs entitled "The Cultural Survival Studies in Ethnicity and Change" is published in collaboration with Allyn & Bacon (the Simon and Schuster Higher Education Group). It will focus on problems of ethnicity in the modern world and how they affect the interrelations between indigenous peoples, ethnic groups, and the state.

The studies will focus on the situations of ethnic minorities and of the indigenous peoples, who are a special kind of ethnic minority, as they try to defend their rights, their resources, and their ways of life within modern states. Some of the volumes in the series will deal with general themes, such as ethnic conflict, indigenous rights, socioeconomic development, or multiculturalism. These volumes will contain brief case studies to illustrate their general arguments. Meanwhile, the series as a whole plans to publish a larger number of books that deal in depth with specific cases. It is our conviction that good case studies are essential for a better understanding of issues that arouse such passion in the world today, and this series will provide them. Its emphasis nevertheless will be on relating the particular to the general in the comparative contexts of national or international affairs.

The books in the series will be short, averaging approximately 160 pages in length, and written in a clear and accessible style aimed at students and the general reader. They are intended to clarify issues that are often obscure or misunderstood and that are not treated succinctly elsewhere. It is our hope, therefore, that they will also prove useful as reference works for scholars and policy makers.

David Maybury-Lewis
Theodore Macdonald, Jr.
Cultural Survival, Inc.
96 Mount Auburn St., 2nd Floor
Cambridge, Massachusetts 02138
(617) 441-5400 fax: (617) 441-5417
e-mail: csinc@cs.org
website: www.cs.org

Preface

This short book is largely a long story. It chronicles the recent history of the Runa, a Quichua-speaking Indian population in Ecuador's Amazon region. The first chapters draw, in large part, on observations from fifteen months of fieldwork in the settlement of Arajuno between 1974 and 1975. At that time, I got to know the Runa as individuals practicing swidden horticulture, who hunted, fished, and lived their created culture while also reacting to external pressures imposed on them by newly arrived colonists and changing national legislation. At the time, the research focused on whether or not the Runa's ordered worldview and lifeways would survive a flood of new neighbors and environmental changes that shifted them from subsistence horticulturists to cattle ranchers. They did.

Beginning in 1979, as Projects Director for Cultural Survival, I had the good fortune to return periodically to Ecuador's Upper Amazon and follow the Runa's adaptation to continuing changes around and amongst them. During this period, their story shifted from the passive to the active voice.

Rather than continue to accommodate to new neighbors and increasing external pressures, the Runa of the Upper Napo organized their disparate communities into a regional federation. Likewise, they shifted their understanding of and response to the old as well as the new political and economic order. After linking to one another as communities in the Upper Napo, they later helped themselves to join into broader, pan-ethnic polities. With this they began to develop a new sense of ethnicity, first as Runa of the Upper Napo and then as Indians of the Americas. The Runa thus became one of the early standard-bearers in what is now a hemispheric social movement—indigenous ethnic federations. These organizations have changed Latin America by successfully thrusting indigenous identities and concerns into the middle of national political arenas that had previously marginalized and stigmatized them.

The Runa's story also has a purpose. It scrutinizes and attempts to analyze the relationship between culture and ethnicity. It would be easy, indeed tempting, to focus on the Runa's mobilization simply as an illustration of a broad regional movement, and thus seek to understand them largely in terms of broad indigenous responses to national, hemispheric, and international political opportunities. Such opportunities have indeed opened and can undoubtedly explain part of the Runa's behavior. However, a singular focus on broad opportunities does not reveal how the Runa interpreted the changes, and thus tells us little of who the Runa now "are." Although their frame of reference has clearly expanded and they have adapted to it, they nonetheless maintain a sense of themselves as a group. This includes their new Indian "ethnic" identity but retains many elements of their unique Runa symbolic frame within which they order, interpret, reflect on, and create their "reality." They thus maintain an active voice in their on-going story, asking us to continue watching them rather than allowing us to shelve it as a finished tale.

ACKNOWLEDGMENTS

The research leading to early chapters of this book was made possible by a grant from the Social Science Research Council. However, the bulk of the information was obtained as part of my work as Projects Director (1979–1992) for Cultural Survival. Though that unique organization is indirectly responsible for the accumulation of the data, an opportunity for which I am extremely grateful, any responsibility for interpretation rests entirely on the shoulders of the author.

Ethnicity and Culture amidst New "Neighbors"

Ancient Dreams and Modern Realities

Overlooking the Pano River in Ecuador's Upper Amazon sits the headquarters of the Federation of Indian Organizations of the Napo (FOIN). The two-story cinder block structure is just upstream from the fork where the Pano mixes with the Tena, then joins the Misahualli and runs into the Napo River. About 100 kilometers downstream, in 1542, the area's first Spanish conquistador and explorer, Francisco de Orellana, also joined the Napo. While he rafted down the Napo and Amazon to the Atlantic, Orellana's chronicler, Fray Gaspar de Caravajal, inscribed into European history and myth such wonders as the Kingdom of the Omagua and the Amazons of Santarem.

As if rechronicling the river's indigenous, or "ethno," history, a mural covers the wall of FOIN's general assembly room with a 500-year progression of Quichua Indian portraits. Families first appear naked, with men holding only spears. Next they are dressed in shorts and tunics, with men packing mail, cargo, and Catholic priests on their backs up from this foothills town to the Andean capital, Quito. Finally, they stand in contemporary Western dress (including eyeglasses), with men carrying briefcases.

Mirroring the final image of this indigenous social evolution, in late 1996 Juanzhu Andi, the president of FOIN, walked past the secretary's desk and into his office. He set down his briefcase and a small plastic overnight bag on his desk. Along the walls were posters from other organizations of the Ecuadorian Andes, Bolivia, Colombia and Guatemala. Indians with chiseled faces and fists aloft announced marches and meetings, proclaimed land rights, and asked for solidarity.

Juanzhu had arrived early, and a bit preoccupied. At 10:30 A.M. he would board the Amazonas bus to Quito where he and other FOIN directors would meet other regional leaders at the national Indian organization, CONAIE, to prepare a joint response to the government's awarding of new oil concessions in the Amazon. After that they had an appointment to meet with a representative of Tritiam Oil and discuss that company's concession, an area surrounding the Galeras Hills on lands claimed by FOIN as its member communities' traditional territory. The second meeting would be difficult—relations were cordial but cautious and responses were uncertain.

Looking northeast out the window toward Galeras, Juanzhu was thinking of his childhood in a small settlement along the Arajuno River where, from a bluff high above the river, there was a clear view of the Galeras. There, he had been told and retold, lived his ancestors as well as spirit beings and wild animals. His mind then drifted to one morning in Arajuno when he was a child of about fourteen.

He remembered that the forest birds had not yet begun their contrapuntal predawn chorus but that roosters were crowing out from houses along the river for the third time that night. Dawn was close. Juanzhu's father, Chuba, was rousing himself. His mother Elena was already squatting beside the hearth and blowing the previous night's embers to flame. Juanzhu and his four siblings rearranged themselves on the family's platform bed, trying to prolong sleep's final moments. Juanzhu pulled down slightly on his blanket and watched Chuba sit up, push aside his blanket, rise, and then go to warm himself by the fire alongside his wife.

"What did you dream?" Elena asked, almost as a greeting.

Chuba quickly engaged her.

"My dream-soul walked beside the river and saw a deer's dream-soul drinking from a pool on the opposite bank," he answered softly.

"Did you shoot?" she asked.

"I grabbed my shotgun and walked slowly toward the deer," he replied. "Then an old man stepped from the edge of the forest. He shouted, "Stay away from my animals!" For a moment, I just stood there staring at him. Then on the opposite bank, I saw a beautiful woman wearing a long black dress and strings of beads—yellow, red, and blue—around her neck and wrists. I waved to her."

"Did she wave back?" asked Elena.

"I think so," he said. "It must have been my spirit-wife. She'll help me. So I kept on walking toward the deer. Then the old man picked up a small stick, shouted again, and hurled it toward me. When I got close to the deer I fired. The animal trembled, stumbled, and then ran into the forest. With the old man still yelling wildly at me, I awoke."

"Was it Iji Rucu again?" Elena said.

"It could have been," Chuba thought.

Women at hearth

Elena knew that Chuba had argued with Iji Rucu about a week earlier. The old man's cattle had wandered into Chuba's new pasture. Chuba wanted Iji Rucu to pay for the damage. Iji Rucu refused.

"I'm not sure," he said. "The dream was not that clear."

As the sky changed to gray-blue, Elena walked to the river to get water. A flock of small parrots flew by, chattering to each other. Dipping a hollowed gourd into the water pot, she offered Chuba a drink. The fresh water would make his soul strong. She too took a swallow and then set the pot atop the fire. When it had warmed, she swirled in some mashed manioc and served Chuba the day's fresh *asua*, manioc beer. He sat, still distracted by his dream. He wanted to hunt the deer whose dream-soul he had wounded.

But on that morning in mid-1974, he could not. This Quichua Indian—or Runa as they call themselves—his compadre Vicente and Chuba's son were to herd Chuba's fifteen head of cattle over to the house of a *mestizo* (mixed race) colonist, José Guerrero. Chuba expected to be there until the afternoon while the veterinarian from the Ministry of Agriculture vaccinated the animals. An interest payment was due to the National Development Bank next month and Chuba wanted to make sure that his cattle were healthy.

When the children arose, Juanzhu, the eldest son, complained of stomach pain. Elena gave him a drink of water, some manioc beer, and a few pieces of smoked peccary meat. Chuba stared at his son and wondered if the stick that had sailed by him in the dream might have gone on to hit Juanzhu. He told his son to rest in bed; Vicente and he would move the cattle by themselves. But Juanzhu got up anyway.

By then it was light, and in the low mist both would have to leave the Runa's world of time and space to meet the vet. He would probably be drinking coffee and talking to Guerrero. Both were from the highland city of Ambato, and because Guerrrero had been living in Arajuno for seven years, he enjoyed the back-home gossip.

Elena slung the tump line of a wicker basket over her shoulder, grabbed her machete and prepared the other children to accompany her in the garden. Chuba and Juanzhu walked along the edge of his pastures, checking barbed wire fences as they walked. Then Chuba's mind again shifted space.

"Who *was* that old man?" he thought to himself. "The images in my dreams are no longer clear. Maybe it *was* Iji Rucu. That old man is different now. When I was a boy, he was like a father. One day, years earlier when this pasture was a forest, he led me to where I shot my first wild bird. He cut off the head, put some blood on my head, and blew on top of it."

As they approached Guerrero's house, the sound of *cumbias* was blaring from the radio. But Chuba's head was filled with the image of Iji Rucu and that bird flailing its wings as it fell to the ground.

Ten years later, Guerrero suddenly sold his house, pasture, and cattle and moved—fled, some people said—to the city. He was confused, even stunned, when Juanzhu and other young Indian neighbors, previously quiet and submissive, formed the local Federated Union of Arajuno Native Peoples. Juanzhu, then about eighteen years old, had finished secondary school and had become one of the young men from villages throughout the Upper Napo who met regularly, discussed the situation of indigenous peoples, frequently dispatched public statements in the name of the organization, and challenged non-Indian intrusion into their lives, land, and resources.

Juanzhu and his peers, though still tied to cattle raising and a changing economy, were different from their fathers. Rather than simply accepting the national political and economic pressures that had pushed his father into cattle raising, Juanzhu and others of the federations were demanding the time, space, and voice needed to adapt.

Chuba, now in his sixties, was not a part of the movement. Though proud of his son, he complained that he was not living with him, expressed a wish that he would help him with in the garden, and griped that the young people "no longer respected their elders" and had forgotten the "old ways."

It's hard to say whether or not Chuba was really upset, or simply reciting the same laments as his father, and his father before him. In some ways, the situation had truly changed. Colonists and similar symbols of government development policies now crowded the Amazon landscape. Related problems dominate much of the regional political life and alter land use and other economic patterns. Yet many of the personal and public images, as well as the indigenous communal patterns that order them, continue to provide Juanzhu and Chuba with the values and norms they use to frame thoughts and plan at least some of their actions.

Their *culture*—the shared ideas and sentiments that generate norms and values—is fluid and adaptable. Though sometimes framed and expressed in images and metaphors drawn from the fauna and spirit world of the rain forest, Runa perceptions are not some arcane set of beliefs that distinguish, distance, and isolate the Runa from their neighbors. They are simply the tools used to create understanding from personal and public experience. At the same time, the Runa's sense of *ethnicity*—the identity created through their relations with other groups—is likewise fluid and adaptable.

This short book chronicles rapid change and analyzes its impact on a single society. Since the 1960s, an expanding frontier has altered much of the social, economic, and political life of Ecuador's Napo Quichua. During the earlier part of this period, Andean highlanders colonized the jungle. The politics of agrarian reform that sparked their arrival altered land tenure regimes and, for many, introduced cattle to their economy. These changes, followed by a rise in regional agribusiness and then oil exploitation, directly and indirectly altered the Runa's perceptions of order and the nature of relationships, personal and ecological, in this rain forest landscape.

Initially, many of the region's Indians responded by accepting a new land tenure regime and related economy imposed by government policy and reinforced by demography. However, in the late 1970s, and in sharp contrast to the Runa's previous responses to their subordinate status (ranging from acquiescence to passive resistance) the region became the earliest setting for a social movement that has now proliferated and evolved throughout much of Latin America and other parts of the world. Napo Quichua were among the first actors in this social movement and have remained principle actors in its evolution toward one of the most broad-based, successful, and least violent "ethnic-based" movements to appear over the past 30 years. In brief, colonization, new tenure regimes, and state political and economic programs sparked the development of the first Indian political organizations, or "ethnic federations" in Latin America and, with them, created much sharper ethnic boundaries and a heightened sense of "ethnicity."

The book also analyzes the impact of these changes on the values and norms through which the Runa organize and interpret their impressions and initiate critical actions. The first four chapters are presented in a way that could suggest a culture framed in such traditional terms as "worldview," "cosmology," or "belief system" and thus could leave the impression that groups who share ideas and sentiments somehow do so in isolation, as distinct "cultural" entities. The Runa have never lived in that sort of isolation. However, the extent and intensity of inter-group relations has increased enormously. Any thick cultural frame gives an inaccurate understanding of the dynamics that have sparked the new "ethnic movement" in the Upper Amazon. Conversely, a focus solely on the politics of that movement and its relations with and reaction to other sectors of society misses the relationship between social action and reflective culture. Many of the local actors would thus be poorly understood, or rather, understood largely within a frame that is not of their making.

To illustrate the culture as well as the inter-ethnic aspects of contemporary Runa life, the book begins with a more focused "local" analysis and then shifts, as the Runa themselves have done, to a broader geopolitical overview. It thus illustrates the tensions and conflicts of people who, in many parts of the world today, quite suddenly find themselves sharing space in a recently broadened ethnic landscape.

In such cases, groups like the Runa must draw on new sets of symbols of communal identity as they become objects of increased public attention. Such changes also provide for a new indigenous sense of self. But that need not replace everything previous. To argue that new conditions and situations require new understandings is tautological. However, it is quite different to explore whether and how some of the Runa's imaging tools and prevailing sentiments remain as others aspects of the society change. As we will see, although marked by a bit of confusion, uncertainty, and disagreement, many of the Runa and others like them have been able to develop a heightened sense of ethnicity while maintaining a unique frame for ordering their more intimate relationships.

In brief, this study does not ask what it "means" to be a Runa. Rather, it breaks down and separates the question by asking what, at present, being a Runa means *for* the Runa—as a sector of an increasingly heterogeneous, local civil society—and *to* the Runa—as a distinct and self-reflective community.

2

Organizing Society: Land, Kin, and Ritual

The Runa of the Upper Napo are one of three Quichua (Quechua)-speaking Indian populations of Ecuador's Amazonian region. About 40,000 strong, some Quichua speakers occupy an area running along the Pastaza river, though most now live in numerous settlements running north from the Napo River to the Colombian border (see Figure 2.1). Until the 1960s, each of the three was clustered by geography and distinguished by dialectical and cultural differences. One group occupied the Upper Napo, another the lower, and a third the Upper Pastaza. Since then, population growth, land scarcity, economic opportunities, and expanded infrastructural development have caused and allowed members of each group, particularly the Runa of the Upper Napo, to relocate in other sectors of the region.

The expressed "hearth" of the Upper Napo Runa is the Tena–Archidona region where towns, settlements, and individual households are spread across a montane region that slopes quickly from the Andes into rugged foothills. Streams cascade through this western sector and flow east into the Napo as it cuts through lower, flatter land and receives the myriad tributaries that meander toward the Amazon (see Figure 2.2).

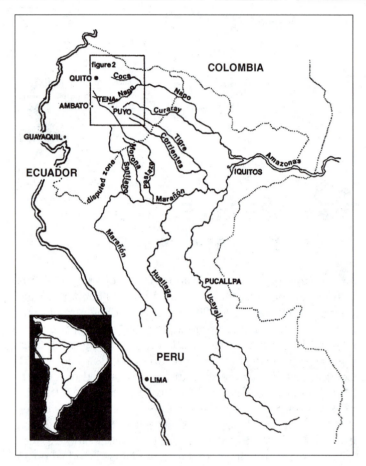

FIGURE 2.1 Ecuador

Moist unstable air, pushed from the opposite direction by prevailing winds, rises rapidly near the Andes. There it condenses and falls as rain throughout the year, drenching the tropical rain forest with roughly 3,000 millimeters annually. This semi-permanent "wet" season is broken only by periods of relative dryness in late January–February and again in August–September.

From the standpoint of human occupancy, this rain forest can be divided into three sorts of tenure regimes (i.e.,

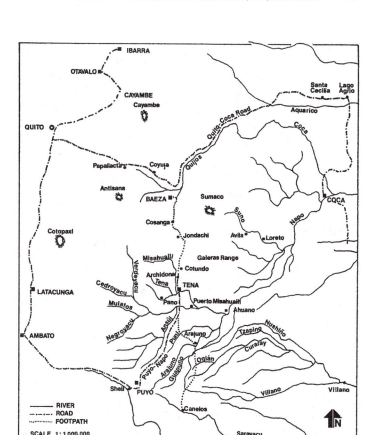

FIGURE 2.2 Upper Napo and adjacent rivers

forms of land and resource rights). There is private property that can be bought, sold, and modified with relative ease; common property that is held by a community and administered through local rules of access and usufruct; and areas of open access that are regarded as no one's property. As with many large but sparsely populated natural areas, those who are not residents (or who pay scant attention to the residents) presume that most of the forest rests on areas of unclaimed open access land.

Prior to the 1960s, the Napo Runa regarded much of this physical space—land, forest, and water—as a patchwork of

Indian "territories" broken only by a few non-Indian settlements. Communities were defined by membership in kin clusters and borders were legitimized by economic use patterns as well spiritual forces, or *supai*. This chapter reviews the Napo Runa's sense of and organization of that "territory" as a physical and social landscape.

COMMUNITY TERRITORY AND SETTLEMENT PATTERN

Boundaries

Unlike the adjacent Andean landscape, where personal plots and community boundaries are marked in ways visible and obvious to Western eyes, the Amazon land use system appears more amorphous. Nevertheless, settlement patterns provide social maps and rules of traverse for the larger expanses of relatively unmodified forest, streams, and rivers. For the Runa, a well-defined gridwork of territories defines their landscape. Though squabbles are inevitable and trespass is common, most land is clearly understood to be in some way demarcated physically and socially. As people use and pass through each other's land, they do so with permission or in violation of rights.

Settlement Pattern

Until the 1960s, most Runa regularly shifted residence across their landscape. Since the seventeenth century, missionaries and others who wished to congregate the Runa regarded their periodic movement as that of an unstable "nomadic" population, incapable of establishing community or congregation, or serving as a labor force. They regularly tried to settle these Indian populations into more permanent and "civilized" settings.

For the Runa, however, periodic movement has been essential. Moreover, it has been ordered and confined to specific locations with carefully defined boundaries. The boundaries that have determined the use rights for garden plots are the most sharply defined. However, there are also rules that guide the use of communal territory for residence, hunting, and fishing. In combination they define a settlement pattern that consists of a minimum of three sites.

Quiquin Llacta

Runa refer to their primary residence as their *quiquin llacta* ("proper" or "true" settlement). These range from small clusters with a few houses to villages of about 50–100 households. A quiquin llacta itself is often marked by a school,

House and garden site by river

chapel, and some form of public building and is identified by proximity to one or another urban area, mission site, or military base. They are generally located along the banks of a river or, more recently, along the road or near an airstrip that serves to link the community to regional political and economic hubs.

Quiquin llacta generally contain the Runa's largest and most heterogeneous gardens, or *chacras*. They also serve as locations for most communal rituals, church services, and schools. People usually move in and out according to the needs and desires of individual families or kin clusters. Prior to the introduction of antibiotics and other forms of improved health care at a local level, any appearance of major contagious diseases—measles, smallpox, and whooping cough—usually produced a sudden and total exodus from the settlement. More recently, communal departures sometimes occur when school was not in session or when someone organizes a large fishing trip. But more often, inter-household squabbles—sparked by offensive remarks; disputes over gardens invasions by a neighbor's pigs or cattle; loose chickens, dogs, or children—fuel social tensions and prompt people to seek respite from disputes. Some Runa simply indicated that, at times, they get bored after a period in one location and seek a change of scenery. Each of these expressed reasons has also been influenced, if not determined, by changes in demography and subsistence needs.

Purina Llacta

For access to additional garden plots or improved hunting, groups of generally one or more nuclear families, travel to what they refer to as their "walking settlement," or *purina llacta*. These are located alongside some small river or stream a day's or more walk from the quiquin llacta and, nowadays, away from the expanding colonist frontier. Houses are generally simple, thatched roof dwellings without walls or floors, but they remain equipped with enough basic domestic utensils to eliminate the need to pack up a household for the trip.

Sacha Purina Pistu

Radiating out from the sacha purina llacta are individual hunting trails, referred to as *sacha purina pistu*. These are trails cut or marked by individuals. The Runa are fully aware of the individual "trailblazers" and are generally respectful of their rights, often restricting hunting to their own trails or those of close kin. Before hunting along another's relatively unused or poorly maintained trail, they generally request permission. For hunting trips along these trails extending over multiple days, the Runa construct temporary palm shelters to spend the night. As population or length of residence has increased within the sacha purina llacta, these temporary shelters have become more permanent dwellings; gardens planted there have increased in size and number. The site thus becomes the equivalent of a sacha purina llacta and the settlement pattern has been replicated. This has permitted expansion and adjustment as population has risen or when social tensions have increased.

In principle, such a pattern can be reproduced indefinitely. However, expansion can continue only as long as there is available, uncontested land onto which to expand. As detailed later, by the mid-1960s, and even earlier in some areas, such expansion had become increasingly difficult as competition for limited land intensified due to colonization from the densely populated Andean region.

Land Use

A common source of confusion, and of many current conflicts over land, is that, for many people, much of it does not "look" as if it used. However, for the Runa and other indigenous people throughout the Amazon region, their land is so carefully managed that outsiders can hardly perceive how it is used. Current research indicates that, despite the image of an Amazonian "virgin forest," the landscape is and has been modified significantly for several thousand years. Balee (1989) suggests that, for agricultural purposes alone, at least 12% of the Amazon has been "managed" and modified by indigenous peoples, and that much of the current mix of species is the direct result of human activity. When one extends "modification" to include semi-domesticated species such as some medicinal plants, housing materials, and hunting trails, an even higher percentage of the land is "managed."

Within a community's territory, land is divided into areas claimed and used by single individuals and families and into other sectors held by the community in general. New members may enter, others may leave, but the territory remains intact. Though boundaries within and between communities are disputed and violated, the Runa nonetheless acknowledge the general tenurial pattern. Access and use are governed by a set of use rules (i.e., rights of usufruct). Though generally unwritten and often unspoken, these rules are widely understood and acknowledged. The sharpest boundaries are those associated with the area's most intensive use. These include house lots, adjacent home gardens, and the larger, most important zones of active food production, the chacras, or their fallow, known as *mauca*.

Garden Lands: Chacras

Chacras, the household production plots, are managed through swidden, or slash-and-burn horticulture. Practiced for at least 5,000 years in Amazonia, swidden horticulture closely mimics the general pattern of natural forest dynamics. A standing forest provides a high degree of equilibrium: predators control pests, tough natural vegetation competes with thorns and weeds, wild plants create chemical and mechanical defenses against insect pests and pathogens. There are also significant "gaps" in the forest canopy produced when trees either die or are toppled by winds. These are filled through natural regeneration from the surrounding forest.

If, however, sectors of forest are extensively or repeatedly cleared for agriculture, pests multiply and their predators diminish, weeds and thorns more firmly establish themselves, and pathogens and insects multiply as they find easy prey in less hardy cultivated plants. By clearing and farming a series of relatively small plots (one-half to one hectare each) and spacing these gardens over a wide area, the Runa minimize many of the hazards. Likewise, through a careful process of plot rotation and extensive fallow periods (fifteen to forty years), they generally have been able to let the forest regenerate and thus prevent the damage that would arise from erosion and leaching after prolonged exposure to heavy rains and tropical sunlight.

Though this pattern of small plots in wide rotation produces a subsequent forest that is somewhat less diverse than the natural forest it replaced, swidden horticulture closely approximates natural diversity. The results are complex polycultural plots, in which diversified plant communities closely resemble the complexity and structure of the natural forest. Allowing for adequate fallow, swidden horticulture is recognized as one of the most ecologically sound, as well as economically efficient, forms of cleared-land use (Balee 1989; Conklin 1957; Irvine 1987, 1989, 1991; Posey and Balee 1989).

In any settlement, community members exercise exclusive rights of usufruct over these gardens on all of the alluvial as well as the older upland soils in and around the settlement. Spacing and demarcation of the plots is, in general, clear and precludes any misunderstanding or competition for resources while a chacra is in full and obvious production.

When a garden is in full production it is dominated by starches—either manioc or plantains. However, diversity within most gardens is extensive; dozens of additional food sources are generally mixed in with main crops. This diversity—again replicating natural forests—controls pests, creates multiple layers and forms of ground cover, and thus provides essential soil protection within the garden.

After the main crops (generally manioc, beans, and maize) are harvested, additional ones (including varieties of plantains, bananas, and fruit trees) remain in production for up to forty years (in the case of fruit trees) and thus mark the property of the individual or the family that initially prepared it. In brief, land use for highly visible, intensive production of starchy staples and subsequent use for tree crops provides a long period of "use" by those who originally planted the area, generally a single nuclear family. These rights can, and often do, continue as the plot is cleared and prepared for another period of intensive use. These patterns of use and rights of usufruct to arable land result in a de facto permanent division of most arable land within a community.

Hunting

Just as the regrowth plot, or mauca, requires a culturally informed eye to define it and to understand the state of its resources, so do hunting areas. High population density and land use patterns near the quiquin llacta and in expanding sacha purina llacta usually lead to sharply decreased fish and game. There are thus quite rigid rules governing the exploitation of these resources.

Spanning out from the riverside household clusters of kin, referred to as *muntun* by the Runa, all forest within two to three hours' walk is considered to be the exclusive territory of the muntun members. In addition, because most hunting trails are cut by individuals or closely related kinsmen, they are used mainly by those who cut them, though there is relatively free access by other muntun members.

Although those outside the muntun are not permitted to freely use the trails, most hunters agree that residents of adjacent muntun can follow game into their neighbor's territory if pursuit is initiated within their territory. However, even in some cases of "hot pursuit," men will stop following game such as deer if they cross what is regarded as the border of the neighboring muntun. Occasional forays into another's hunting territory usually do not produce sanctions, provided that the intruder does not attempt to hunt the trails regularly. But if someone suspects that a member of a neighboring muntun is consistently encroaching on the territory of another muntun, indirect criticism is usually the response. However, if incursions continue, threats of induced illness through shamanism or other acts of retribution are frequently invoked.

As distance from the settlement increases, enforcement of boundaries is less rigid. When a dispute occurs within a "buffer zone" or "no mans land," it quickly becomes a source for dispute resolution and more rigid boundaries result. In some cases, boundaries are defined unilaterally when a single muntun lays claim to an area it is currently using. Generally, however, boundaries are set by mutual agreement.

As detailed later, Runa territorial boundaries—their sense of political geography—are understood to be coterminous with the domain of the muntun's focal shaman's spirit helpers. For example, after a series of disagreements of hunting rights among members of two muntun, the focal shaman of each negotiated new llacta boundaries without offending either party's sense of pride. They met, drank the widely-used hallucinogen *ayahuasca* together, and called in their respective spirit helpers. These spirits indicated the areas in which their animals roamed. The shaman thus defined their community domains by invoking mutually acceptable external mechanisms to evaluate these infringements.

Fishing

A community's riverine territory is understood to include the space from one recognized point (e.g., mouth of a river, stream, or deep pool) past the settlement or quiquin llacta itself to a similar, easily identified downriver area. Fishing rights here are rigidly enforced; this includes exclusive rights to hook and line fishing, gathering and netting, as well as dynamiting. But for large fish poisonings, neighboring groups are often invited, largely because enforcement near water is relatively easy compared to an outsider's foray into distant forest.

Stunned fish usually pass through the territory of more than one muntun. People complain bitterly if dead or stunned fish pass through their territory when the residents are unprepared to gather them. Consequently, if a muntun anticipates large-scale fish poisoning, it is assumed that they will invite all other muntun through whose territory the poisoned fish will run.

Violations of fishing territories produce stronger protests than those occasioned by violations of hunting territories. On at least one occasion, when a large group of men were fishing on the nearby river, one of the party was bitten by a snake and died shortly thereafter. Those who accompanied the man before he died agreed that the snake must have been sent by a powerful shaman from the downriver settlement. That muntun regarded the river as their "territory" and had warned the people to stay away. Several other deaths were explained by mentioning that they had occurred shortly after the individual had been caught panning gold on another's section of the riverbank. Even if the death occurred months after the threat, it could be interpreted as punishment for a territorial violation by one community against another.

Kin Structure and Organization

Membership in, and thus rights of access to, resources within a communal territory are defined in terms of a group referred to as a *muntun,* or "cluster." This, the Runa's principal organizing unit, is a residential group generally composed of several overlapping kindreds (i.e., a kin group that is oriented in terms of the individual rather than, for example, through a lineage or clan).

The kindred often clusters around a powerful shaman, the focal point of most muntun, and many carry the name of that shaman as the group's marker. The site of a particularly powerful shaman is therefore a residential attraction.

Consequently, though all Runa males state that, all things being equal, they prefer to live with their parents and brothers and thus to bring their wives there (i.e., virilocal residence), such decisions are complicated by phenomena such as resident shamans. Because such factors are rarely equal, residence choice varies widely and groups range in size from small clusters of brothers and their wives to large groups linked by a more varied web of kin. Consequently, Runa frequently maneuver and manipulate kin categories and status to locate themselves within particular groups.

In large part, the stimulus for manipulating kin ties comes from the efforts of individuals to incorporate themselves into a particular muntun and to create for themselves appropriate statuses within that residence group. Such concerns illustrate the significance of the muntun as a residential unit and as a community.

If virilocal residence were somehow imperative rather than simply preferential, the muntun could be either a localized kin group or a kin-based local group. Male members of an *ayllu* or consanguines, and members of a muntun would be largely the same. But because many men opt for uxorilocal (wife's family's) residence and devise complex strategies to cope with the structurally subordinate status that implies, they appear to be more concerned with their residence than with their proximity to ayllu members.

The Runa thus distinguish between groups based on ties of kinship, syllu, and kin groups based on ties to locale, muntun. From the standpoint of social organization, the distinction is critical. In localized kin groups, it is kinship that unites the group. In kin-based local groups, kinship is an idiom for inclusion into a social unit where other concerns may dominate (e.g., access to property, proximity to water, and as we shall see, essential links to a focal shaman.)

Anthropologists such as Leach (1961) argue that such material concerns often outweigh ties of kinship. For the Runa, the structure of kinship serves as an idiom for ordering positions and defining a wide network of relations. The muntun provides the economic base (access to land and resources) and a critical set of social ties that encourage the activation of those links. Thus a Runa's position is determined not simply by being part of a kin group but by using a set of widely understood structural rules to gain entrance into certain kin-based groups that have particularly appealing characteristics. Analogous manipulation of the structure of ritual for social and political ends, as detailed in the next section, clearly illustrates some of the same priorities for ordering one's position within this social space.

RITUAL AMONG THE RUNA: THE MARRIAGE CEREMONY

The Runa's principal rituals surround marriage. Three formal events—*tapuna* (request), *pactachina* (fulfillment of agreements), and the *bura* (wedding)—punctuate a lengthy process through which a group acquires a wife for one of its members. This ceremonial sequence dramatizes the efforts of the groom's family (collectively referred to as the *cari parti*) to impress and demonstrate respect for the bride's family (collectively referred to as the *huarmi parti*). Marriage ceremonies, when described as stylized cultural phenomena, are ordered dramatic performances in which music, dance, and costume combine to enact images of idealized social order and balanced reciprocity.

By contrast, when the Runa recall specific ceremonies—tapuna, pactachina, and bura—that they have attended, there is little mention of the ritual structure. Description usually focuses on the behavior of the bride's father, the *huarmi yaya*. Although his role is framed and constrained by ritual structure, he creatively orchestrates critical activities during each ceremony. The choices and decisions he makes support the primacy of the muntun and reflect his concern for a high-status position within that kin-based local group. This section first outlines the formal structure and then illustrates its individual dynamics.

Tapuna

The tapuna (also called the *maqui churana,* the clasping of hands) closes a betrothal. After a bride is selected, the groom's family frequently probes the attitude of the bride's family. If the girl's family responds favorably, a tapuna is organized. Emissaries, or go-betweens—usually a husband and wife referred to as *parinu* (male) and *marinu* (female)—are generally selected as the ritual sponsors for the entire ceremonial sequence that can last up to a year or more. On the day of the tapuna, these solicitors try to arrive at the prospective groom's house before dusk, when the entire family is most likely to be at home. Kneeling outside the entrance, they explain why they have come and ask permission to enter. Once inside the house, they give gifts of clothing, food, and drink. They continue to demonstrate respect through highly formalized requests until the family formally accepts the offer.

Pactachina

Following a long, communal hunt for wild game for the feast, the parinu coordinates with the hosts and invites the guests. On the designated day, the guests gather at the bride's family's house. The groom's parents and their helpers gather in a nearby house. The parinu selects helpers—a *tucadur* (violin player) and a *virisidur* (a combination drummer and chanter)—who will perform throughout the ceremony. A married couple, called *cumpaña*, are selected by the groom's family to aid and accompany the marinu and parinu during the dancing. During the ceremony, the male cumpaña wears a rectangular piece of white cotton cloth, called *cushma*, with a slit in the center for the head to pass through. The female cumpaña wears a shawl over her shoulders, tied and pinned in the front. Regardless of its color, it is said to be white. The marina also wears a white shawl, or she may wear one of mixed red and white. The choice, it seems, is dictated by the availability of cloth. The parinu always wears a white cushma beneath another of either pure red or mixed red and white. Both men wear hats.

When the cari parti has gathered in their house, the parinu initiates a dance. He, the marinu, and cumpaña then move to the center of the house and form two lines. These male and female lines move backward and forward in short shuffling steps. The pace, gradually increasing, is established by the drummer.

Meanwhile, cari parti helpers set up a cooking area outside the house and begin to prepare the feast. Large, hearty bowls of soup are circulated. The bride's father checks each bowl—to make certain that each has an ample portion, they say—and then directs it to one of his guests. After the guests have eaten, the virisidur begins to chant to the cari parti, inviting them to dance. As he sings, the marinu and the female cumpaña move among the cari parti guests, encouraging them to dance or simply (and laughingly) dragging them into the dance area. By late afternoon, when hosts and guests have finished eating and dancing, the formal aspects of the ceremony have ended. Everyone sits down to talk and to continue drinking throughout the evening.

Bura

As with the pactachina, the groom's family must first accumulate game and must purchase some additional items such as bottled drinks and candy. They then inform the bride's family that the cari parti is ready for the bura. Unlike the previous ceremonies, the bura takes place in the groom's family's house. In most other aspects, the ceremonial process is nearly identical to the pactachina except that, at this final event, the bride and groom are present and active participants.

The Wedding Ceremonial Sequence

The most visible dramas of the marriage ceremonies are enacted by the cari parti. The huarmi parti, by contrast, are passive recipients or, at most, mild critics of the performance. During the *maqui churana* sequence, the parents of the groom present gifts and humbly express their obligation to the bride. This ceremony involves only a man and his wife communicating with another man and his wife about their respective offspring. The pactachina that follows is a more inclusive and dramatic metaphor for the ideas expressed in the maqui churana. As it raises the request for alliance and balanced reciprocity above the level of the nuclear family to one that includes the two ayllu, the pactachina duplicates the structure and sentiment of the tapuna. As an intermediary stage in the sequence, it also initiates a rhythmic pattern of interaction and conjunction that remains unfulfilled until the bura ends the ceremonial sequence. Like lines of polyphony, the ideas and emotions expressed in the pactachina and bura are reiterated in several different and complementary "voices." The "voices" are visual, locational, and verbal.

The marriage costumes visually demonstrate opposition and balance. The basic contrasts—red and white—represent respectively, the huarmi (female) and cari (male) sides. The cumpana are members of the groom's family. They aid and support the parinu and, as such, are representatives of the cari parti. They dress entirely in white, the male in a cushma and the female in a shawl. The parinu and marina play a different role; they represent intermediaries. By dressing in a pure white cushma covered by another of either red or mottled red and white, they are consistently intermediate and neutral, symbolic and active links between the intermarrying ayllu.

The bride, as she dances before her ayllu, is unmistakably huarmi parti. She wears pure red. Her costume also reinforces the idea that the ceremony is performed before the huarmi parti. She is thus as much an intermediary as is her spouse. But as an actor performing before her ayllu, she demonstrates herself as one of them, not to be forgotten or subsumed as an intermediary.

The dance rephrases and repeats the message conveyed by the costumes. The dance concisely and clearly demonstrates the anticipated outcome of their efforts. Ayllu members dance in opposing lines of males and females, dancing back and forth in unison and to an increasingly rapid pace rhythmically regulated by the virisidur and tucadur. It is the drama of ritual coitus for the newly married couples and the symbolic conjunction of two ayllu.

The location of the event in the ceremonial sequence also illustrates the symbolic absorption of the bride into the husband's group. Both the maqui churana and the pactachina take place in the home of the bride, and both ceremonies dramatize efforts of the groom's family to please the bride's family. There is no mention of the bride leaving her natal home. The bura, during which the bride becomes a part of her husband's group, takes place in the groom's natal household and thereby signals the bride's change in residential status.

A running narrative complements the visual, gestural, and locational imagery of the ceremonies. The chants explain the actions of both parties, proclaim their virtues, verbalize the cari parti's good will, and set the emotional tone for the events. With word and music, the virisidur describes a context that combines beauty, balanced reciprocity, respect, and alliance. This is the ideal world and these are the sentiments associated with it that the cari parti tries to create through the ceremonial sequence.

The wedding ceremonial sequence has been described as it would be seen through the somewhat passive eyes of the huarmi parti. The huarmi parti's guests appear only as observers of the cari parti performance and as recipients of cari parti hospitality. But, while the hosts sing and dance for the huarmi parti, a simultaneous and more subtle performance is underway as well. This one lacks the predictable order and tradition of the alliance ritual. As a spectacle, it does not dominate the ceremonial arena, but as a carefully considered and executed social act, it commands the attention of all the guests.

The huarmi yaya can manipulate the ceremonial context and thereby briefly allow himself to express and even alter his social status. Guests at a particular ceremony rarely scrutinize or criticize the gifts presented by the cari parti. They usually focus on the huarmi yaya's selection of guests, the order in which they are acknowledged, and how the gifts are distributed. In each case, the huarmi yaya attempts to weigh the obligations of general hospitality against his efforts to secure or improve his situation within the muntun through selective treatment of his guests. His behavior is one of the most significant social and organizational aspects of these public events.

The huarmi yaya invites all of the guests. Almost all invitations occur among members of the muntun, and most muntun members expect to be invited to such ceremonies. He also seats them. The bura, unlike the events that precede it, takes place in the cari parti residence. Invariably, there are numerous onlookers, for no one wants to miss the excitement of the event. Although the huarmi yaya would never remove the uninvited onlookers, he must carefully seat his guests so that no one feels neglected or isolated.

The guests' entrance frequently occurs in such an irregular manner that it becomes impossible to immediately seat all of the guests in appropriate positions (i.e., to separate male and female huarmi parti guests). Without actually designating seats for each of his guests, the huarmi yaya regularly surveys the assemblage to make sure that none of the invited guests sits outside the main circle.

During the feast, members of the cari parti rush back and forth from the cooking area, picking up bowls full of soup and carrying them to where the huarmi yaya stands. Having surveyed the entire food supply earlier, the huarmi yaya inspects each bowl to make sure that it has the proper amount of meat and fish. If he is not satisfied, he may ask the server to add more. Some Runa say that the purpose of this is to make sure that each guest receives a the same amount of food. However, most will admit that the huarmi yaya is actually making sure that all of the guests receive an adequate portion while, more importantly, making sure that some guests are fed particularly well.

In addition to approving the size of the serving, he also determines the order of distribution. He first serves those whom he wishes to impress or to show particular respect. Although the guests sit around in a circle and could easily be served in rotation, servers criss-cross the floor and distribute soup in an order determined by the huarmi yaya. The guests easily observe the huarmi yaya's priorities because there are generally never more than four or five bowls, so some guests must wait until the more favored have finished.

Throughout the serving, and despite exhortations by those from the cari parti to be festive, the huarmi yaya must remain sober. That is, he must maintain control over his thoughts and actions. At the same time, he cannot consistently refuse to drink for this would offend his hosts. He must maintain a delicate balance between happiness, openness, acceptance and sobriety in order to manage the event successfully. Thus, he tries to drink as little as possible until the formal aspects of the ceremony have ended.

The final formal stages of any pactachina or bura come when the huarmi and cari parti dance as groups. While simultaneously emphasizing their autonomy as an ayllu, the dance is also an opportunity for the respective groups to publicly display their friends and supporters. At most ceremonies, the division of people into their appropriate parti is quite clear-cut. Sometimes, however, the affiliation of certain guests is unclear and they can be recruited for dancing by either parti.

Such situations are particularly noticeable with regard to powerful shamans at weddings that link two groups within a single muntun. At one wedding, a shaman who had been invited by the huarmi parti was also a close friend of those of the cari parti and helped them to hunt the meat for the ceremony. When the two groups took turns dancing, the cari parti danced first, as usual. As they worked to draw dancers onto the floor, the cari yaya called to the shaman to come and dance with them. The huarmi yaya then moved quickly to stop this and insisted that the shaman was his guest and could not dance with the cari parti. The huarmi yaya had been careful to assure that the shaman had received priority in both the order and quantity of food distribution, and he was thus anxious to have his generosity reward by the shaman's symbolic acknowledgment of allegiance to the huarmi parti.

The ceremonies reveal how muntun dynamics can heavily influence the ceremonial process. Ideally, the huarmi yaya would grasp the opportunity to either demonstrate or improve his status. Although many of the individuals may be close kin, coresidence is the critical bond; nonresident kin need not be invited, and low-status resident kin are often not accorded preferential treatment. The ceremonial context allows the huarmi yaya to strengthen his ties with valued compadres, formal friends and pre-existing affines as well as consanguines. The primacy of the muntun in social hierarchy is particularly noticeable with regard to the focal shaman. The following chapter considers the spiritual factors that would promote the importance of the shaman. These illustrate the importance of the focal shaman and his role in motivating the strategies and decisions outlined earlier.

3

Symbols for Understanding Self and Social Order

When Runa describe the world, their cosmos, they generally render an image with four distinct planes—*Ahua Pacha* (the Upper Lands or heavens), *Puyu Llacta* (an intermediary cloud layer), *Cai Pacha* (this land—its earth, forest, and water), and *Ucu Pacha* (the Under World). Communication or movement between levels is, they say, minimal and appears to exert little effect over daily life. Similarly, their mythical accounts recite the events that first ordered the cosmos and produced the current life and landscape of the Upper Napo, but this imagery does not inspire daily life, influence decisions, or shape critical imagery, either private or communal.

By contrast to the Runa's apparent indifference toward the distant layers of the universe and their genesis, Cai Pacha is a regular locus of discussion, debate, interpretation, questioning, fear, and curiosity. It is the arena for social relations and other public acts, the stimulus for personal beliefs and private motivations, the space of life and death. It is the world of the quotidian, as well as ambiguous events and situations that provoke curiosity and invoke a spiritual world. By drawing from and building on a repertoire of symbols and metaphors, the Runa carry out their personal and public search for order and understanding. Equally, the underlying values and sentiments inspire and stimulate personal decisions and social actions. This chapter first outlines some of the symbols of and for personal identity and public order, and then it illustrates how such symbols are used to create, recreate, and modify that order.

Cai Pacha is a horizontal plane covered mainly by rain forest, rivers, flora, and fauna. Dotting that surface are diverse communities—the Runa, their indigenous and non-indigenous neighbors, and, they say, *supai* or spirit beings. The boundaries of this multi-ethnic, multi-being landscape are distinct yet porous, with regular movement in and out.

Until recently, most Runa "became" distinct people largely within the boundaries of their own ethnic group and their specific muntun. Forays into the domains of their indigenous neighbors, non-Indian colonists, and the supai are filtered through and thus reinforce much of the understanding derived from the community. As will be detailed later, beginning in the early 1960s, state policies and an influx of non-Indian colonists realigned the Runa's ethnic boundaries, redefined their public identity, and expanded their sense of community. Nevertheless, many of the symbolic interpretive frames outlined here remain and continue to inform the Runa's understanding of indigenous social order and the reciprocal rights and obligations required to maintain that arrangement.

Like most people, the Runa attempt to organize uncertainty and comprehend experience through personal and communal signs and symbols. These also form the basis for expressing and creating the norms, obligations, and expectations that motivate social action as well as shape epistemology. These "working" beliefs are dynamic and highly subjective. Yet like the wedding ceremonies reviewed in the previous chapter, they are sufficiently ordered to suggest a shared cultural and value system.

Patterns of reciprocity—the give and take of social life—illustrate many of the Runa's norms and values. Though the general process of reciprocity is broad and universal, its patterns are nonetheless spun around a particular cultural or symbolic frame and set of values.

For the Runa, a recurrent theme is illustrated by their explication of significant personal interaction and critical social relations. These are expressed either as positive or negative affective ties that, in turn, generate the understanding and expression of norms. Critical "encounters," they say, produce either antagonism or cooperation. Others, though equally revealing of norms, priorities, and social boundaries beyond their intimate community, are more emotionally neutral and thus fall outside the paradigm.

The theme is a metaphor that can be stated something like this: "Personal knowledge derives from interpersonal intimacy." Intimacy, in turn, often demands nearly complete identification with some "other."

To develop fully, the Runa say that they must periodically but temporarily transform themselves into various "others." When these "others" accept and acknowledge this transformation and identification, they transfer essential knowledge and power. The events range from straightforward personal interactions to highly symbolic spirit encounters and dreams in which ambiguity complicates interpretation. Though each set of experiences is private and intimate, they are often described and interpreted publicly. The community and the individual join to determine the affective meaning. Personal imagery is thus shaped by communal symbolization.

BECOMING A RUNA

Much of a male Runa's personal growth is a spiritual process in which stages are neither abrupt nor marked by public rites of passage. One gradually "becomes" a Runa, a personal self, through regular, individual, existential experiences interpreted as signs of the acquisition of power and skill. The process is a series of unique, idiosyncratic experiences woven through personal imagery. However, they are shaped by a frame of widely accepted logical and emotive beliefs without which individual experiences would probably be meaningless to other members of the community.

Musqui

Personal identity begins when elders transfer to children, through demonstration and subsequent symbolization, essential knowledge and skills that they refer to as *musqui*. There is a *tarabana musqui* (the capacity to labor diligently at difficult chores), an *aichahua apic musqui* (the ability to catch fish), a *purina musqui* (the power to walk long distances rapidly), and a *sacha purina musqui* (the ability to hunt successfully in the forest without fear of animals or forest spirits).

They are acquired through symbolic transfer by one of the senior members of the muntun who transfer part of their inner being, referred to as *samai* (breath). The donors transfer a portion of their total musqui. Recipients claim that they would never attempt to acquire more power than the donor intends to impart, otherwise he would be seriously weakened. Even when an elder is extremely ill, considers himself close to death and accepts the total loss of his musqui, men claim that they would not request all of a man's musqui. Death, they say, might ensue more rapidly. Because donors are their friends, it is best to let these friends die slowly and naturally.

The affective bond between donor and recipient during musqui acquisition is a critical and characteristic feature. Most men remember those who transferred musqui to them and often state that the elders helped them "out of affection" or "because the old man liked me." Such relationships can bind members of the muntun in a manner that reinforces and cuts across age and kinship ties and creates lifelong links, even when no close kin ties exist.

Testing the Musqui

Proof of a sacha purina musqui requires a solitary hunt as a test of courage and skill. For some, if the boy brings game he is considered to have acquired the musqui. For others, acquisition of the musqui is a more complex, mystical experience that involves an encounter with a supai. Here a vision confirms the acquisition of the musqui and also initiates a pattern of interaction that, if properly managed, can lead the boy toward a higher stage of personal intimacy in which he is linked to the world of the spirits.

RELATIONSHIP BETWEEN RUNA AND FOREST SPIRITS

According to the Runa, supai are beings who occupy and maintain control over the forest and the rivers that surround Runa settlements. Supai can mediate relations between Runa and forest wildlife, and in many instances can assist in disputes among the Runa themselves. However, this support is understood to be contingent upon intimacy and affection. The following is an account of an adolescent male's first solitary hunt as related by the boy's father.

Several muntun members and I had transferred part of our musqui to Juan since he was a infant. One day we built a small hunting blind on the edge of one of our chacra. The next day, shortly before dawn, I gave Juan the rifle and told him to go to the blind and wait for game. He said that after about two hours in the blind, he noticed an agouti [a large rodent] and got ready to shoot. At that moment, the blind began to shake and the ground began to tremble. Juan saw a figure coming toward him. He said it resembled a priest with a long dark beard and black garments. He picked up the gun and ran home. He lay in bed for the rest of the day. When I returned home in the afternoon, we talked and I tried to get him to tell me about the encounter. I wanted to know whether or not the supai, or whoever it was, had blown on or over Juan's body. But he could not remember.

The concern with gaining intimacy and proximity is clearly illustrated by the following account in which Cuchi, felling trees near his sacha purina llacta, suddenly heard his hunting dog yelping in the forest. He grabbed his rifle and ran toward the noise. Soon he saw a large anaconda, about four meters long, coiling around his dog. The constrictor then moved toward Cuchi, who fired into its head and killed it. He first severed the head and placed it in his bag. Then he skinned and salted the body, hoping to sell the hide. While removing the hide, he cut into the internal organs and, to his surprise, numerous anaconda fetuses spilled out.

He buried the boa's head and began to fast—no *aji* (chili pepper), salt, hot foods, or sexual relations with Runa women. However, the fact that the snake was a pregnant female disturbed him. Now, he said, instead of taking over a male *amarum's* woman he would have to contend with an angry widower.

The following night, he said, a pair of boa women visited him in his dreams. They were affectionate and anxious to sleep with him. He was quite nervous, for he wanted to gain their friendship and respect. Yet he hoped to avoid conflicts with, as Cuchi put it, the "husband." When the women appeared in his dreams, Cuchi stressed to them that he was not afraid of the male's revenge and, in the dream, he displayed a large dagger that he said would defend him. At the same time and equally important, he explained that he had killed the amarum only to protect his best hunting dog. Cuchi also apologized for having salted the skin while it dried because, he said, the amarum huarmi might be angry with the way that he had desecrated the flesh. Salt, as noted above, is alien to the supai world.

By controlling his interpretation of dream imagery, Cuchi projected himself as a brave male, but he also showed himself to be a considerate, sensitive, and respectful individual worthy of the support and admiration of amarum huarmi who could teach their skills and transmit their powers over animals. To expand his personal power, he temporarily transformed himself into one who was accepting, sympathetic, and empathic with the values and habits of the amarum supai.

Supai llacta, or spirit settlements, are located in the interior of notable geographical features such as swamps, hills, riverside cliffs, and deep riverine pools. To illustrate, one man told how, as he dreamed, his soul entered a pool near the mouth of a stream that ran down the slopes of Pasu Urcu into the Arajuno River. He said that once inside, it was like a city with wide main streets and narrow side streets. Beings, some of whom looked like Runa and others who looked like Catholic priests, wandered in the interior, appeared at the windows, or stood in the storefronts.

The forest is littered with such habitats, and the Runa agree that most fish and game live in supai llacta. The resident supai control the movement of birds and animals that range within defined territory controlled by their masters. Runa explain that, just as a male and female human might own a flock of chickens, a pig, several dogs, or perhaps some cattle, the supai possess wild animals. The forest is conceived as a patchwork of spirit estates (*llacta*) and their surrounding forest domains.

To establish initial and, from the Runa's point of view, essential relations with forest spirits, the Runa have adapted models of interaction and reciprocity, patterns of etiquette that are variations of the initial paradigm. These parallel relations developed during musqui acquisition. The Runa say that supai, like elders, require and expect—demand, in fact—that a socially mature Runa demonstrate a submissive and empathic attitude toward these "others." To reward such efforts, the spirits share knowledge and give power. Building on respect and affection, a Runa can become continuously stronger through the aid of these donors.

With elders the affective bond is easily perceived, but with supai the Runa must filter ambiguous individual experiences and private imagery through the affective paradigm to understand each experience. However, after this degree of personal relationships with a supai has been established, an individual is regarded—and regards himself—as a possessor of spiritual knowledge. This status, defined by the term *yachaj*, or "one who knows," is the final stage in the musqui acquisition, but it can also be an intermediate step toward closer relations with spirits and, thus, a higher degree of personal development. While the status is held largely by men, the general belief system is shared by all Runa.

Once a Runa male establishes a relationship with a supai huarmi, the huarmi tries to draw him farther into her llacta. However, spirit women's knowledge and power are limited. The supai huarmi acts as intermediary between a Runa and a pantheon of other supai who can do personal favors far beyond simply providing access to game. This frequently includes aid in causing and curing illness or causing death.

Intimate friendship with a wide range of supai greatly expands the power of an individual within his social as well as natural environment. As a Runa becomes "friends" with

powerful supai, they share game within the area they dominate. Properly established, a relationship with a supai can
enable an individual Runa to exercise considerable control
over movements of animals within the sector of forest dominated by the specific supai and allow that person to draw on
that spirit for support in curing or causing illness and death.

A powerful supai will not accept an individual as an intimate simply because he has been introduced by a supai
huarmi. One must work to improve the relationship with increased sensitivity, respect, and effort. The overall pattern,
however, is familiar—it involves food prohibitions and a variety of prescriptions. But to "take the other" with more the
powerful supai also requires ingestion of hallucinogens
(principally ayahuasca, or *Banisteriopsis caapi*). Its bitter taste
and powerful visions are closely associated with the diet of
powerful supai. In turn, by contrast to the widely understood and somewhat uniform techniques used to initiate relations with supai huarmi, friendship and identity with
powerful supai require behavior tailored to the personality
of the individual supai.

Acting as intermediaries for the supai, elder shamans
dictate the nature and duration of fasting, teach the unique
songs of each supai, explain the etiquette required for proper relationships, and administer the intake of hallucinogens.
Thus while working to achieve intimacy with powerful spirits, a developing Runa, generally a male, must gain the respect and friendship of a master/strong shaman, a *shinzhi
yachaj,* as well. When a Runa completes his education and
training with a specific shaman, he is considered to share
the master yachaj's knowledge as well as the knowledge of
that man's most intimate supai.

Runa often describe a particular yachaj as "having studied under" such-and-such a supai. They agree that the
power of an individual yachaj increases with the number of
supai with whom he has studied. However, friendship and
intimacy with shamans and, by association, their supai is
said to be more important than breadth of experience.

If two shamans simultaneously request another shaman's or supai's aid, the latter will go to their more intimate
friend. A yachaj who has achieved intimacy with a wide va-

riety of supai is regarded as a shinzhi yachaj. He is considered superior to one whose experiences are less deep and broad, the latter referred to as a *yanga* or ordinary yachaj.

These ideas, and illustrative episodes, concisely illustrate the affective bonds that are essential to individual growth and the development of critical social ties. The manner in which the symbols are shared illustrates and shapes the sentiments that, in addtion to kinship, link those who share these symbols and sentiments to form an ideologically integrated social body.

ORDERING LIFE THROUGH DREAMS

Becoming a Runa, to the point where one is a person of knowledge or a yachaj, means drawing on symbols for understanding the norms and rules of reciprocity and thus providing a frame for experience. Symbol systems, however, have an "intrinsic double aspect: they give meaning, i.e., objective conceptual form, to social and psychological reality both by shaping themselves to it and by shaping it to themselves" (Geertz 1973:93). The Runa's use of symbols likewise influences and shapes, as well as reflects, social action. That is, while serving as models *of* reality they are also models *for* reality.

Dreams

As much as, if not more than, any other medium, the private and public manipulation of dream images illustrates how symbolization creates order and gives form to the complex, subjective, and otherwise confusing relationship between ideas, images, and events.

Dreaming is also understood to be part of social life, not simply a form of reflective internal drama. Interpretation is used to predict hunting and fishing success, foreshadow illness and death, contact supai, and comprehend social relations. The ability to dream clearly, act decisively in dreams, and remember dreams is said to be characteristic of a strong and capable person. The Quichua terms *ali* or *shinzhi muscuyuj*, good or strong dreamer, are the only antonyms for the term *chiquiashca*, the state of "uncleanliness" that inhibits an encounter between Runa and supai. Dreams therefore illustrate another projection of the affective paradigm used to frame interpersonal and spiritual growth. In dreams, however, the images are cast into more complex settings that shape communal as well as personal actions and decisions.

Dreaming is understood as an activity of souls, *alma*. While the body rests, the soul leaves and wanders in an environment where the borders and restrictions of waking life are diminished. Dream souls can travel great distances, enter strange places, and interact with either human, animal, or supai souls.

Actions that take place during this time are understood to initiate a chain of events that continue into waking life. Dreams are not simply forecasts of future events that must be stoically accepted. Individuals, the Runa say, exercise considerable control over events during and after dreams; it is important to remember dreams in order to act upon them after waking.

There are many common dream images and interpretations. Dreams of water suggest personal strength; dreams of large flying objects indicate successful hunting. For such images, discussed apart from any social context, individuals can simply recite motifs and standard interpretations.

However, when a dream interpretation is understood to provide insight into some personal, emotional, or similarly significant event, a more elaborate, subjective, and intense analysis occurs. Though dreaming is private and personal, interpretation is frequently communal. Public interpretation often helps to shape the content of dreams only partially remembered, suggesting events or relations that, they suspect, the dreamer might have "forgotten." Such dreams are "expressive for the individual dreamer as representations of unconscious mental processes, but are also communicative, since many dreams are verbally described to other people and indeed are known primarily by such mechanisms" (Firth 1973: 217). Interpretation, therefore, is the created product of both a dreamer and his or her public, each focusing on and filtering images. Together they draw on and contribute to the knowledge of those involved and to an understanding of the broad social and emotional context of the dreamer.

Images are often understood to be spirits whose souls wander in dreams and interact with other forms of being. Though initial contact with a forest spirit woman often occurs during the day and follows a period of fasting, encounters with her also take place in dreams, as illustrated by the following account.

> I was walking with a friend. We were inside Pasu Urcu, the hill across the river. Inside the hill is a city just like Quito with houses, stores, music, windows, and all sorts of people. As we walked along, a beautiful woman with long black hair and beads around her neck and wrists approached us and asked me to follow her. I left my friend to go with her. Then she asked why I had not come to marry her earlier and said that we must go to her mother to ask permission.
>
> I was very nervous but I followed her nonetheless. She quietly explained to me how I should approach her mother and what I should say to her. Then we came to a big door and opened it. After passing through three sets of doors, we entered her mother's room. She sat on an huge bed, hunched over with her face to the floor. But her body was covered with bristles, like a porcupine.
>
> The young woman nudged me.
>
> "Say something!" she said.
>
> I said I was afraid.
>
> Finally she told me, "Tell her that you want to marry me."
>
> I did.
>
> "You can't marry my daughter!" the mother said. "She is born of the *huayusa* [an herbal tea]. To live with her you would have drink much of it."
>
> "I too drink huayusa and would drink whatever amount she offered," I said. Then the old woman lifted her head and a pair of dark glowing red eyes stared at me.
>
> "If that's true, then you can marry my daughter," she said.

We then left and I woke up. That was how I met my supai huarmi.

Dreams, Shamanism, and Conflicts

Men often begin to hunt one another in the same way that they begin to hunt animals—in dreams. The Runa rarely kill one another in open feuds. Much of what they call "warfare" occurs in dreams. It often begins, they say, when a shaman tries to injure or capture a wandering soul.

Indirect attacks, using another's soul, are understood to be the most frequent method by which shamans attack wandering souls. To avoid witchcraft accusations, their attacks are usually carried out by *suldadu*, helpers of the shaman. Suldadu can be either supai whom the shaman has under his control or influence, the souls of those Runa who accompany the shaman while he takes ayahuasca, or any other soul that the shaman has captured or commandeered while its owner dreams.

Men of the Arajuno muntun described how, by joining the shaman during hallucinogenic experiences, they voluntarily traveled with him on his attacks. Others remembered that their souls had been involuntarily captured by other shamans. Some even confronted the shaman to complain of such robbery.

Suldadu are not always readily identifiable. They can mask their identity, as the following dream illustrates.

Many years ago I dreamed that my two sisters and I were walking up the trail from the river to my house. Suddenly several men dressed in military uniform came running after us. Hoping to escape, I grabbed my infant sisters and ran until we reached the tall tree which now sits beside my pasture. Then I grabbed my chair. In my dreams during that period, I owned a beautiful chair which could fly me wherever I wanted. So I sat down in the chair, grabbed my sister Adela and put her into my lap.

But there was no room on the chair for my other sister, Lisa. Adela and I took off over Pasu Urcu and flew north until we reached Huama Urcu, near Pano. We flew inside the hill and saw all of my relatives who had died long ago. My grandfather came up to greet me. He told me that I was very strong and said that after escaping such an attack I would surely live a long time. Several months after the dream, my sister Lisa died, her stomach distended with bile.

Interpretation often requires detailed discussion and analysis to determine whether the attack is aimed directly at the dreamer or indirectly at the focal shaman of his muntun. Once this is determined, they have to consider who might have sent the suldadu and why they might have done so.

Such interpretations are obviously highly subjective and variable. When startled awake by violent dreams, Runa will sometimes rise, no matter what the hour, stoke the fire, and remain awake to prevent their soul from wandering back into danger. Others, those shinzhi muscuyuj who are confident of their ability to perform in dreams, say that they purposely go back to sleep, hoping that their souls will once more wander into danger as it provides an opportunity to test themselves.

Shaman are not invulnerable; they do not cause and cure illness without risk to themselves. The retaliation precipitated by dreams of shaman attacks, mentioned earlier, illustrates the complex social consequence of symbolism.

To identify the guilty shaman and determine his motivation, dreams and hallucinogenic experiences help to frame complex and unordered impressions and emotions. Once a shaman is suspected, the Runa usually attempt to sanction him in some way. Runa sanctions are usually administered indirectly and symbolically, using supai intermediaries to attack dream souls or carry deadly *biruti* (magical darts) to the victim. These symbolic sanctions can cause significant emotional and interpersonal strain.

Sanctions against shaman can occur even in the absence of illness or death. The yachaj's latent power makes him a continuous suspect for potential danger. This fear, combined with the frequently expressed desire of established shaman to eliminate competition, produces an environment in which the shaman's life is continuously in danger. Younger yachaj emerge gradually and only reveal their status when their confidence and training have reached a relatively high level.

The Yachaj and the Muntun

These accounts illustrate the focal shaman's principal role in his muntun. At the same time, they help to account for his unique status within that group and exemplify the initial paradigm's pervasiveness. Without such a powerful protective figure as a shaman to support the muntun, most Runa feel that they have little chance of surviving another shaman's attacks. They see the focal shaman, aided by his supai intimates, as the provider of health and personal security for his muntun.

The same supai account for the shaman's unique capacity to control the local fish and game that are essential for the muntun's subsistence. The shaman, who derives his power through warm affective ties with supai, projects that power onto the muntun with the same warm affection. Despite the shinzhi yachaj's superior capacity to manipulate a complex symbolic system, the focal shaman is not a power figure who arbitrarily withholds and dispenses his powers. He cures whenever he is asked. Shaman and non-shaman alike say that shinzhi yachaj consistently provide personal and material support out of love and affection for members of the muntun. All shaman can and do perform cures for individuals outside of the muntun but, in Pasu Urcu for example, the focal shaman emphasized that he called upon his most powerful supai friends only to cure members of his own muntun.

The muntun members see their relationship and accompanying sentiments toward the shaman in a similar manner. The shaman frequently needs them and, out of love and respect, they say, muntun members invariably reciprocate the favors that the shaman dispenses. On a symbolic plane, they accompany him during his hallucinogenic voyages. At such times, men regard themselves as the shaman's "soldiers" who support and protect the yachaj as he attacks or cures.

In summary, the shinzhi yachaj, or focal shaman, is the individual within a muntun who has extended his personal development farthest into the world of the supai. With such singular knowledge and intimacy, he—to a greater extent than any other individual—can rely on the supai for support and aid.

The muntun members, in turn, need the shaman's support for basic subsistence and personal protection, they will usually support him during his frequent struggles with other shamans. Both sides of this balanced, complementary relationship conceive of their links within the same paradigmatic frame—as long-term, personalized affective bonds— that guide the interpretation of numerous aspects of Quichua social and cultural life.

Throughout the course of Runa enculturation, both cosmology and social relations function reflexively; private symbols often obtain their meaning from public phenomena and subsequently stimulate social action. The belief system also mirrors, reinforces, and shapes the patterns of ecological adaptation and social organization outlined earlier.

Ecological, social, and epistemological factors are gradually interwoven in the following manner: while the acquisition of a sacha purina musqui guides a boy into the world of the forest and animals, he also learns general territorial concepts and specific boundaries claimed by his muntun. These general and specific concepts of territoriality are subsequently reinforced by supai contacts that always occur within the circumscribed muntun territory; the Runa learn that muntun territory and supai territorial limits are coterminous. While personal development strengthens concepts of territoriality, this enculturation also defines and maintains patterns of social organization.

Muntun membership is therefore essential. However, status differences amongst focal shamans vary considerably. These differences frequently influence a Runa's choice of muntun affiliation and help to explain the manipulations that pervade muntun organization. The shinzhi yachaj, in turn, require the support and protection of their local residence group. Such vital reciprocity motivates and perpetuates a high degree of muntun solidarity. Dream interpretation demonstrates that culturally defined symbols, not just economics and social organization, help to order and influence social action within the muntun.

Neither the ecology of the Upper Napo rain forest, nor the economic patterns used to exploit this area, nor the kin ties that bind the inhabitants, nor the belief system that draws from and adds to all of the other influences, determines the structure and process of Runa society independently. It is the complex interaction of each element—environment, economics, social relations, and worldview—that generates their sense of society.

The Runa, thus far, suggest a rather closed society, as if they exist as some sort of isolated island unto themselves. The review has focused largely on relations among the Runa. Likewise, their concerns and needs, generally expressed in term of these relations, center on power, reciprocity, and sentiments framed largely in terms of interpersonal ties and the social positions created among the Runa. In brief, this review focuses on their culture more than their relations with other groups. This, in many ways, reflects their situation until the 1960s. To a large extent history allowed them a degree of isolation in which they focused more on each other than on other groups. In a sense, they have placed their ideas and concerns with ethnicity in the background. This, as will be detailed throughout the remainder of this book, is not their current situation. As also will be detailed, this internal focus on values and sentiments has not become some lost "traditional culture" either.

A group's focus, or primary emphasis, changes at any particular historic moment. This, as we shall see, has happened on the Upper Napo. Ethnicity has moved into the foreground in many communities and for many individuals. However, it would be misleading to neglect their more inwardly focused attention and sentiments as somehow secondary concerns. To consider only the external influences and subsequent relations with outside groups suggests that public, inter-group relations somehow define existence and thus not only precede private beliefs and sentiments but also determine their essence.

In brief, historical and demographic conditions vary and exercise different degrees of influence. Such forces always operate, so they preclude any idea of groups as cultural isolates frozen from the influence of time. Nonetheless, the Runa, at certain times and in certain places, have paid greater attention to themselves and their relations with each other than with the influence of outside forces on their society.

Understood thus, the previous chapters are not an effort to somehow enclose Runa society—that is, to deny the role of history and to suggest that there is some intrinsic and pervasive sense of self and society that defines the group or precedes any external influence, or that some essence precedes their existence in the formation of self and society. Rather, the description illustrates and emphasizes the Runa's focus at one particular time. Prior to the 1960s public ethnic boundaries existed and undoubtedly helped to shape their world. Yet for largely demographic and historical reasons, these boundaries were not so sharp nor so highly circumscribing as to demand the degree of attention to external influences that now dominate much of their life, as shown in the remaining chapters of this book. The current need to distinguish themselves from some "other" encouraged but did not create the Runa's sense of self and space. This is something they developed more self-reflexively. Some of their ideas and beliefs have changed dramatically, but their unique organizing frames and processes of symbolization have not disappeared as external pressures have increased, gradually since the late nineteenth century and rapidly since the 1960s.

4

From Apu to Patron

Prior to the late nineteenth century, travelers, government officials and missionaries violated the Runa's space on Upper Napo only sporadically. Non-Indians had relatively little impact on the indigenous residents' social and economic life or the land and resources they needed to sustain it (Macdonald 1979, Muratorio 1991). However, just before the turn of the twentieth century, occurrences far from the Upper Napo River indirectly altered and intensified relations between the Runa and non-Indians. The stimuli for such change emanated from opposite directions and, depending on whether one's attention is focused downriver toward the Amazon or upriver toward the Andean highlands, the influence offers a striking contrast.

To the east, the port of Iquitos mushroomed into a large-scale export center as tons of crude rubber floated in on motor launches and dugout canoes that linked gathering stations throughout the upper Amazon. Fanning out from the gathering stations, Indians collected the crude rubber for bosses, *patróns*, who worked these employees under conditions that ranged from debt servitude to slavery. Paradoxically, to the west in the Ecuadorian highland and coastal regions, a "Liberal Revolution" led by Eloy Alfaro produced legislation designed to remove longstanding abuses of the Indian population.

The Runa of the Upper Napo did not experience the full impact of either development, but both changes indirectly generated a powerful and pervasive system of patron–client ties that dominated inter-ethnic relations for several decades. Previously, religious and government officials known as *apus*, or authority figures, dominated most inter-ethnic relations. The shift from apu to patron increased the Runa's participation in the national economic structure and thus strained the socioeconomic patterns and belief systems outlined in the previous chapters. These historical events produced the model for patron–client ties, led to new legislation that favored the rise of the patron, and defined the impact of the patron-based economy on indigenous society.

THE RUBBER BOOM

During the final years of the nineteenth century and the first decade of the twentieth century, the Amazon forest provided the raw material for all the rubber demanded by a rapidly expanding world market. The Amazon rubber trade also produced enormous profits, due largely to an overworked and underpaid labor supply. As the demand for rubber increased, merchants traveled up and down every tributary in search of rubber trees and Indians to tap and drain the trees.

The brutal excesses of the infamous Peruvian Amazon Rubber Company have been described by travelers in the early 1900s who journeyed up and down rivers near the major ports of Iquitos and Manaus and provided firsthand accounts of greed and sadism (e.g., Hardenburg 1912). In many areas, labor conditions worsened as the first decade of the twentieth century drew to a close; crude rubber production diminished through overexploitation at the same time that demand rose rapidly. To meet increasing demands, the Peruvian Amazon Rubber Company forced Indian laborers to increase production, leading to widespread abuses.

Casement (1912) eventually exposed the sadistic and exploitative excesses of the Peruvian Amazon Rubber Company. His description, which largely portrayed working conditions on the Putumayo, is often regarded as typical of the entire Upper Amazon (e.g., Collier 1968). Though the rubber boom led to exploitative and deplorable working conditions throughout the Amazon, labor exploitation was less blatant in the upper tributaries some distance from the areas easily navigated by motor launch, as these were marginal to the large-scale marketing centers.

Rubber on the Upper Napo

The limited number of written and oral accounts of the rubber boom on the Upper Napo River indicate a situation that ranged from passive patron–client relations to forced labor and obligatory population shifts. However, the more violent forms of labor acquisition appear to have been rarely used. Runa from the Tena–Archidona area recall this threat but mention that Peruvian troops never advanced as far up the river as Puerto Napo, Tena, or Archidona (Macdonald 1979, Moratorio 1992).

By contrast to the widespread reports of kidnappings along the Putumayo, Napo Runa accounts mention that they traveled as far as the Madre de Dios River in Peru, but never as captives or slaves. They were simply accompanying patrons. However, due largely to competition between the smaller Colombian and Ecuadorian merchants and the large-scale entrepreneurs of the Peruvian Amazon Rubber Company (supported by the Peruvian army and government), workers were sometimes captured or otherwise restrained by Peruvian officials (Bravo 1920: 129–130).

Although some Runa employed by rubber merchants were lost in downriver labor turmoil created by the Peruvian Amazon Rubber Company, most Indian gatherers did not travel far from their home territory. They gathered rubber without being uprooted from their principal settlement, as patrons acquired this labor through debt servitude.

Debt Servitude

Debt servitude, or debt peonage, centered on a patron's acquisition of labor or raw materials through a system of debt-related obligation. In most cases, the patron first gave small, inexpensive gifts to the Indians. He later escalated the value of his presentations to include cloth, axes, and shotguns. These were paid for in rubber, which the Indians gathered from areas where the patron exercised exclusive exploitation rights. In most cases, the Runa were unaware of the market value of either the goods they received or the rubber they traded. Nor did they understand the mathematics involved in weighing the rubber. The situation was ripe for abuse. Merchants demanded high prices for their goods, paid little for the rubber, and manipulated their books so that debts were never eliminated.

In an effort to eliminate some of the abuse, the practice of obligatory receipt of gifts was declared illegal by the *Ley de Oriente* (1899). However, unlike the *apus*, government authorities, who first established this *repartimiento* of goods, the patron defended his presentations by citing the legal, contractual nature of the relationship.

Institutionalizing the Patron

The rubber boom ended abruptly in 1912 when Malaysia began production of plantation-grown rubber. Unable to compete with Malaysian efficiency, Amazonian rubber production dropped rapidly. Though Runa reported that rubber was collected in eastern Ecuador long after 1912 (demand again increased sharply during World War II), it never reached the scale of the early 1900s. Nevertheless, the rubber boom produced the onset of a form of patron–client relationship that continued along parts of the Napo River until the 1960s (Muratorio 1992).

ELOY ALFARO AND THE "LIBERAL REVOLUTION"

As patron–client ties progressively dominated inter-ethnic relationships in Amazonia, political events and legislation originating from the more populous Andean and coastal regions of Ecuador indirectly aided these new ties by eliminating competition for Indian labor. In 1895, a liberal government with General Eloy Alfaro as its *Jefe Supremo* forcibly took power in Ecuador. In reaction to the abuses of power, restrictions on personal liberties, and effects of intense regionalism that accompanied a long period of Conservative Party political control, the Liberals wrote a new constitution and enacted a series of new laws. The Catholic church was one of the first institutions to be affected. Although the Liberals' first constitution (1897) recognized Catholicism as the official Ecuadorian religion, there was an unmistakable thrust toward secularization of the government. The Liberals' second constitution (1906) declared an absolute separation of church and state. The Catholic church, long accustomed to sharing power and influencing policy, opposed the new government from the start. Resistance from foreign clergy led to the expulsion of the Jesuits from the Upper Napo in 1905.

Church accounts portray this period as one in which the docile Runa were robbed of their protective shepherds and then exploited by rapacious patron "wolves" (Spiller, 1974: 17–19). Yet in 1892, the Runa stormed the Jesuit mission at Loreto, captured several missionaries, and set them adrift in canoes down the Napo River. The Catholic clergy blamed local non-Indians for inciting the violence, claiming that the whites resented the church's progressive work. Accounts by local Runa, on the other hand, reported frequent whippings and other forms of physical punishment meted out for their failure to perform tasks demanded by the clergy. The expulsion of the Jesuits thus removed one source of power and control from the Tena–Archidona region. Only government officials and non-Indians remained to exploit indigenous labor.

When the Liberals stemmed the church's power, they also diminished government abuse of Indians. Among a series of new laws, the Liberals enacted legislation in 1895 that exempted Indians from taxation and thus ended despised and abused tribute payments. This "Liberal Revolution" thus restructured patterns of exploitation by enabling patron–client ties to supersede other forms of asymmetrical relationships.

However, patron–client ties were not simply a form of or means for economic exploitation or social manipulation.

RUNA AND PATRONS

In many cases, the Runa entered willingly into these new relationships. These patron–client ties are perhaps best understood in terms of a "moral economy" (Scott 1976, Thompson 1992). This "economy" includes a broad set of relationships that carry a complex frame for interpreting relationships and creating patterns of interaction that define norms and rules of reciprocity regarding rights to land, resources, and the fruits of production. Though imbalanced and exploitative, the "whole person," face-to-face nature of patron–client ties structured and guided interaction, and thus framed a symbiotic social order generally perceived as acceptable.

Economic Role of the Patron

The authority structure imposed by the presence of the apus and priests was based largely on the Indians' perceived obligation to accept their legitimacy as representatives of large, powerful, supra-local institutions. By contrast, the Runa frequently initiated subordinate ties with patrons. This was in part because the patron became the primary supplier of essential material goods.

In the Ecuadorian Oriente, such goods as shotguns, powder and ammunition, machetes, and steel axes had long been essential imports (Harner 1962, Oberem 1971:98). Likewise, salt became a commodity that was acquired exclusively from patrons. Although it had previously been acquired through trade from Peru's Huallaga River, border disputes gradually decreased trade with groups from the Lower Huallaga salt deposits. Trade ended in 1943 when the Peru–Ecuador War left the borders heavily guarded (Oberem 1974:355).

Cloth too became a commodity obtained mainly from patrons. Runa bearers, commissioned by religious and government officials, had previously obtained personal supplies of cloth and other manufactured goods by hiding them amidst their commissioner's cargo. However, when the *Ley de Oriente* (1899) prohibited forced, unpaid transport and required payment of indigenous labor, merchants sought to cut costs by using alternative transport systems. Improved roads made transport goods less labor dependent. In the early 1900s, roads and mule trails began to penetrate the Upper Napo. By 1921, a mule trail extended from Quito to Papallacta and, in the opposite direction, from Archidona to Jondachi (Jaramillo 1964:31–32). By 1931, mules could travel from Quito to Baeza (Holloway 1932:122). As the path improved, two muleteers and several mules could inexpensively transport the loads of thirty to forty bearers. As mules came to be used more frequently, the number of indigenous bearers diminished. Previously, the trip had been an arduous ten-day climb and a six-day descent. Men who acted as bearers for these trips reported that, as the period of the patrons began, they made fewer trips to the highlands, and then they only carried goods across territory not yet penetrated by improved roads and more efficient transport systems. By the 1930s, Indian bearers entered the urban areas much less frequently.

In summary, improved transportation gradually decreased the need for bearers and thus decreased the incidental trade that took place during these trips. Roads, motor vehicles, and mules indirectly increased indigenous dependence on patrons as their only suppliers of essential manufactured goods.

Sociopolitical Role of the Patron

The patron also served as mediator or broker between the Indians and institutions or individuals of the non-Indian society. Travelers to the Oriente consistently mentioned that patrons provided them with canoe men and guides from among their clients. The patrons also brokered relations with national and local civil authorities. Runa frequently mentioned that patrons were essential when Indians had legal problems. Many Runa believed that the police were employed by the patrons (because police often captured and punished recalcitrant debtors). Runa thus sought out their patron whenever they became embroiled in civil disputes or legal action. Indeed, from their point of view they needed a dependable and influential patron to represent them.

Selection of Patrons

Patron–client ties were dyadic relationships that served to bind pairs of individuals through a set of mutual obligations. In the Upper Napo River area, such sets were established when a client established a debt with a patron. Writers such as Beghin (1963) and Spiller (1974) have emphasized the exploitative nature of debt servitude and portrayed the Runa as helpless victims, totally subordinate to the patrons, and incapable of escaping their oppressive situation. Although debt servitude was undoubtedly exploitative and Runa did attempt to escape debts, in the Tena–Archidona area there were at least a dozen patrons competing with one another for Indian labor. Each patron was well-known; Runa frequently discussed their personalities and their treatment of clients as factors that served as criteria for selecting patrons.

Muntun members generally established relations with the same patron. Those who took up residence in a new muntun frequently also tried to establish ties with their new muntun's patron. Thus, although each patron–client tie represented a single, dyadic relationship based largely on economic dependency, Runa did not search out the most economically advantageous arrangement. Muntun affiliation determined the selection of patrons. Patrons often named a *capitán* (captain) from each muntun to act as their intermediary with other members of the muntun. Familiar with aspects of indigenous social organization, the patron often named captains from among the dominant authorities within the muntun, often the focal shaman. The captain was often asked to pressure recalcitrant debtors and make them appear before the patron. Periodically, captains gathered men and women to perform labor on the patron's hacienda. For this, the captain received preferential treatment from the patron.

Patrons and Patterns of Runa Society

The institutionalization of the patron system altered the form of inter-ethnic relations among the Runa. As permanent residents, patrons established more regular and intimate contact with the indigenous population than did the governors or priests who irregularly resided in the Oriente. Liberal legislation stifled government and church exploitation of Indians and thereby permitted the patron to dominate inter-ethnic economic ties. As indigenous trade networks provided fewer and fewer manufactured goods, the patron became the principal supplier of such items and, in turn, the principal recipient for most valuable raw materials. Because he mediated the exchange of manufactured goods and raw materials, he also became a vital intermediary between the Indians and the local and national authorities.

In addition, labor performed for the patron did not lead to a radically different lifestyle for the Indians in the Upper Napo. Neither the nature of the work nor the time allocated to perform it demanded a drastic reallocation of their time and energy. Panning for gold and laboring for short periods on haciendas were easily accommodated into the dominant, subsistence-based mode of production.

As such, patron-oriented labor did not alter the previous residence pattern. Patrons did not control exploitation rights to land; they only controlled the workers. Individuals were not assigned locations along a river where they were told to gather gold or rubber; all they had to do was to turn over such products, wherever they obtained them, to the patron. Likewise, existing concepts of territoriality, which served to control exploitation of fish and game, were easily extended to include the search for gold. Rights of usufruct were limited to the exposed shorelines within each llacta, and encroachments by outsiders were sharply prohibited.

Finally, labor expended for the patron did not radically alter the Runa's existing schedules or other aspects of their resource and time allocation. Neither gold panning nor occasional labor on haciendas was so time-consuming that they precluded existing economic activities. Because rubber and gold were gathered from nearby llacta territories, the Runa were able to accommodate gardening, fishing, hunting, and gold panning into a relatively flexible schedule. The demands imposed by the patron were not so extensive as to require full-time efforts, but only a minor shift in their allocation of time. Such chores did not dominate the economic pattern and therefore did not replace the dominant mode of production. Likewise, although the patron–client relationship constituted a shift in the social relations of production, it did not eliminate the existing patterns of social organization and prestige.

In summary, for the Runa, the patron caused a readjustment of indigenous life, but their social and economic patterns and the beliefs that generated that society remained relatively unmodified. There were no significant reallocations of their time and resources; rescheduling was minimal. The mode of production described earlier thus remained dominant. New forms of social relations that characterized the Runa's link to the national social and economic structures required adjustment to only a small part of the overall sociocultural pattern. Much of this was to change throughout the region during the 1960s. Here we detail that change through a case drawn from one Napo Runa community called Arajuno, the settlement of Juanzhu and Chuba and the one from which many of the cultural ideas and expressions outlined earlier were drawn.

5

Colonists, Land Reform, and Cattle: A Case Study

THE SETTLEMENT OF ARAJUNO

1920–1960: Oil Exploration

Arajuno, now a town of about 1,500 people, became a quiquin llacta of the Napo Runa during the 1930s when a shaman, Quilluma, and his muntun gradually converted their purina llacta to a more permanent residence on the left bank of the Arajuno River. At the foot of a hill called Pasu Urcu they built shelters on uplands that stood above a large sector of more recent alluvium, known as the Isla, which they used for intensive garden plots. Arajuno had been Quilluma's purina llacta for several years, as it was for his entire muntun. There they had panned that section of the river for their patron, Ester Maldonado. They fished in the Arajuno River and hunted the forest on the left bank only. They considered the opposite bank of the river to be the western frontier of the hostile Huaorani (Auca) and were therefore hesitant to set up permanent residence there.

Within a few years, spectacular changes in the landscape occurred on top of a sandstone bluff that faced Quilluma's settlement across the river. Axes cleared the forest, tractors leveled the land, and stones from the river filled in wet, swampy soil. This construction was part of a project that was initiated in 1921, when the Leonard Exploration Company received a concession for petroleum exploration in the Ecuadorian Oriente (Galarza 1974:111, Tschopp 1953:2304). In 1937, the Ecuadorian government ended Leonard's contract and gave the Anglo-Saxon Petroleum Company (subsidiary of Shell Oil Company) exclusive petroleum exploitation rights in the Oriente.

By 1938, Shell Oil Company began constructing an air base on the left bank of the Pastaza River where it cut through the Andean foothills. In the following years, they searched for oil throughout the Oriente and eventually dug six wells and built five airstrips to service them. In the mid-1940s, two of these wells were drilled near Arajuno, one at the head of the Vuano River and the other near the head of the Nushino River. Between 1944 and 1945, Shell constructed an air base on the flat bluff opposite Pasu Urcu. With it came a permanent staff of over two hundred men—British, North American, Dutch, and Swiss administrators and technicians, as well as highland Ecuadorian laborers and office workers (Frank Bellew, personal communication).

Merchants from the highlands were attracted to the area, where they set up small stores and saloons across the river near Quilluma's settlement. Several men from Quilluma's muntun worked for the company for short, three-month periods and were released before the company became obliged to provide social security and severance pay. During this period, all of the Arajuno Runa expanded their gardens in order to sell surplus manioc and plantains to the oil camp.

Within five years, the oil camp was abandoned without having produced any petroleum (Galarza 1974:132–154, Tschopp 1953:2304). The Ecuadorian army arrived, dismantled most of the buildings, and floated the lumber downriver. For the Arajuno Runa, five years of oil exploration provided some short-term employment, but it did not alter their traditional lifestyle. In fact, the well-armed presence of the oil camp guards, who protected the camp after Huaorani speared an employee, gave the Runa the security to expand their traditional territory and establish purina llacta in the interior of the opposite bank. These sites, the Oglan and

Nushino Rivers, then became the principal purina llacta of the Arajuno muntun. The Runa also reported that during the period, despite large numbers of men, few of them hunted so game supplies were not severely depleted. Following the departure of the oil camp and the merchants who supplied it, the only non-Runa to visit the settlement was a fundamental Protestant missionary who had established a permanent camp near the mouth of the Arajuno River and occasionally travelled upriver to Pasu Urcu. By 1955, a permanent Protestant missionary family lived across the river from the Pasu Urcu settlement. Although they established a school, maintained a small medical dispensary, and attempted to convert the Runa to Protestantism, until the 1960s their principal focus rested on the Huaorani, an uncontacted and hostile Indian population who lived to the east of Pasu Urcu (Elliot 1957, 1961; Wallis 1971, 1973).

The Huaorani were seen as one of the few remaining, untouched "heathen" frontiers for Protestant missionaries. Arajuno, being the closest settlement accessible to Huaorani territory, served as a springboard for initial contacts and, later, as a staging area when permanent missionaries established themselves among the Huaorani in the early 1960s. Only after this contact did the missionaries direct their attention towards the Arajuno Runa. At the same time, due largely to the access and security provided by the missionary presence, colonists began to arrive. Catholic missionaries then settled on the left bank of the Arajuno, and a new lifestyle developed among the Runa.

The 1960s: Colonization

Early in 1960, Uquillas Tutin and his son Ruben left the town of Shell and rode a bus north along the Puyo–Napo Road as far as construction would allow—about thirty kilometers. From there they began walking northeast through the forest toward Arajuno. They got lost and wandered for three days before finding their way back to Shell.

On their second attempt several weeks later, they located the Puni River, headed north–northwest to the Arajuno River, and eventually arrived in Arajuno. They explored the settlement for three days and returned to Shell. Their clumsy arrival in Arajuno marked the onset of a series of events that radically transformed indigenous social and economic life there; Uquillas and Ruben were the vanguard for thirty families who were preparing to enter Arajuno as colonists. Several local and national events precipitated that transformation.

These first colonists did not stumble into Arajuno accidentally. When the Shell Oil Company maintained operations near Arajuno, the elder Tutin worked as a supplier for the company. Fifteen years later, his experience served to convince the colonists that fertile, unclaimed, and abundant land existed in Arajuno. The colonists were told that a road was about to be cut through the forest and connect Arajuno with more developed areas. This would eliminate the settlement's isolation that demanded a two-day walk from the nearest road and required that all heavy objects be flown in expensively by Shell-based aircraft.

With such encouragement, thirty families inscribed themselves within the Instituto Nacional de Colonizacion and formed the "Colonia Carlo Julio Arosemena," named to honor the Ecuadorian president and also in the hope that his namesake, the colonia, might receive some financial support. The colonists were a disparate group who had left the Andean highlands several years earlier to settle in the Oriente as either independent agriculturists or employees. Tutin and his son worked at a tea plantation near Puyo. Freire, another founder of the colony, was a carpenter who helped build a Protestant missionary hospital near Shell. Most of the potential colonists also claimed and farmed land near Shell or Puyo, but their plots were small and Arajuno seemed to offer better opportunities.

For a year after the first visit, the colonists traveled back and forth to Arajuno where they selected land and planted subsistence plots. In late 1960, forty-eight males and one female arrived to settle the colony. To establish a baseline for their settlement, the new colonists selected two stone roads that had been constructed by the Shell Oil Company on the right bank of the Arajuno River.

This side of the river was unoccupied, save by one Protestant missionary family. Few of the Runa regarded the new colonists as a threat or a dangerous encroachment on their territory, despite the fact that most of the Runa had originally lived near the city of Tena where they had witnessed a progressive dislocation of Indians. The new arrivals were settling on land that, the Runa said, was threatened by Huaorani attack, even though Protestant missionaries had been living peacefully among the Huaorani for three years. Assuming that the colonists would act as a buffer and deterrent to attack, most of the Runa welcomed the settlers. Unopposed, the colonists cleared the growth away from the roadbeds and settled along the roadside. They then invited topographers from the Instituto Nacional de Colonizacion to enter Arajuno in order to measure and assign lots. At this point, the Runa's attitude changed. The Runa realized that Pasu Urcu had become part of the same expanding colonist frontier that forced the Indians out of Tena.

If legal titles to land were distributed only among the colonists, the Runa realized, they might eventually lose all claims to their land. They approached the resident Protestant missionary and the newly arrived Josefine Catholic missionary to ask for their aid and support in acquiring land titles. At the time, both missionaries were openly competing for converts and were violently denouncing one another, so each agreed to support the Runa in hopes of acquiring local spiritual dominance.

Initially, each missionary suggested that the Runa request communal (global) titles for large tracts of land that they would exploit as church-affiliated cooperatives. The Runa, having witnessed several unsuccessful cooperative attempts near Tena, rejected this suggestion and insisted on individual lots. When the topographers arrived, they measured the land and assigned fifty-hectare lots to most heads of households.

Measuring and dividing up land in Arajuno was one thing, but obtaining legal title for the land was another matter. When the topographers departed, they left receipts for 14,000 sucres (about 700 dollars) that they had received to cover legal and other processing fees for the land titles. The money was turned over to a representative of the Instituto who took it to Quito. Neither he nor the money was ever seen again. Disillusionment increased when the road to Arajuno never materialized. By 1963, the reputation of Julio Arosemena had changed from populist leader to public drunkard, and he never responded to requests for aid from his namesake colony. As a result, they changed the name from Colonia Julio Arosemena to Colonia Arajuno. This only accentuated their isolation and, in general, the future of the colony appeared much less promising than it had in the early 1960s.

The original colonists gradually abandoned Arajuno, and by the mid-1960s only eight families remained. They clustered on the lots closest to the airstrip, which greatly reduced the amount of land they originally claimed. Several abandoned lots were later occupied when five families from the southern highland province of Azuay settled in Arajuno. One of them had met a few of the remaining Arajuno colonists and, sparked by their glowing descriptions, persuaded several relatives to accompany him to Arajuno. Like the original settlers, those from Azuay quickly became disillusioned by the isolation of the area. Within two years, all had left.

In 1967, a second group of surveyors arrived and began to measure lots. This time they were sent by the Instituto Ecuatoriano de Reforma Agraria y Colonizacion (IERAC), which replaced the Instituto Nacional de Colonizacion in 1964. Again the colonists, hoping that land titles would finally be granted, fed and housed the surveyors during their stay. But the survey was meaningless; the colonists later learned that the surveyors were only undergoing training in Arajuno. Land titles were finally granted after a third survey team visited Arajuno in the late 1960s.

In January 1969, another colonist group arrived—thirty families from the highland province of Loja. A severe two-year drought in Loja province led them, like many other small farmers, to resettle throughout Ecuador. Aided by the sympathetic provincial governor, these Lojanos were given basic supplies and flown into Arajuno. As with all other settlers, they were told that land was abundant and fertile, that land titles would be granted, and that a road was about to be constructed. As usual, the land titles were delayed and work on the road was never initiated. Following the pattern established by the other colonists, the Lojanos gradually abandoned Arajuno. By the early 1970s, only five of the original thirty families still claimed land in Arajuno, and several of these were only seasonal residents.

Thus from 1960 to the early 1970s, fifty-five to sixty colonist families had settled in Arajuno. Of these only eight remained. But in less than a decade their comings and goings stimulated changes in local land tenure patterns that transformed over 3,000 hectares of communal land into individually owned lots. Colonists claimed approximately 400 hectares; the Runa owned the rest. Aroused by a large-scale influx of colonists after which few settlers remained and threatened by a dispossession that never materialized, the Runa quickly became landowners. Most of Arajuno was parceled into individual lots.

The Runa's success in acquiring land titles was atypical for the Upper Napo. Among the Indians, the national agrarian reform agency, IERAC, was infamous for its failure to provide Indians with secure titles to their land. Two factors, however, aided the Runa of Arajuno. First, although the Indians initiated the effort to acquire land titles and demanded individual ownership of their holdings, they were consistently supported by both Catholic and Evangelical Protestant missionaries. They had supported the initial surveys and, by frequently pressuring the provincial and national agrarian reform offices, aided in seeing the land titles legalized. Second, colonist and Indian land was surveyed at the same time. To hand over titles to one segment of the population and not to the other would have been a blatant demonstration of preferential treatment. In addition, there was no scarcity of land near Arajuno.

The Isla

Despite radical changes in the overall pattern and concept of land tenure in Arajuno, many aspects of the previous use system persisted. The Isla, the settlement's highly arable alluvium, was not subdivided into individually owned lots. Earlier and unsuccessfully, the Catholic missionary, in efforts to establish church-affiliated communal land holdings, claimed a large plot of land that included the Isla. In turn, even though the Runa scrambled for individual lots, they allowed the Isla to remain and be worked as communal land with individual rights of usufruct. This supported the missionary's efforts to prevent subdivision and satisfied both parties.

The local priest, who had always hoped to congregate the Runa close to the mission, realized that their regular visits to the Isla's garden plots adjacent to the mission (the mission was located on *rucu sacha*—old, relatively infertile land—just above the Isla) would facilitate contact and control. The Runa, in turn, were anxious to maintain usufruct rights to the Isla, the best alluvium soils for swidden horticulture and thus the principal site for subsistence plots since the muntun had settled in the area. By contrast, the lots located on the opposite bank and closest to the Protestant mission were entirely old uplands and thus less fertile soils. The lands never sparked any interest in being developed as communal land holdings. The Isla was therefore demarcated and declared as a communal but totally secular garden territory.

In summary, beginning in 1960, new concepts of land tenure transformed Arajuno. Previously, as a member of the muntun, anyone could claim usufruct rights to one or more garden plots along relatively restricted zones of recent alluvium close to the riverbank. One could also exercise hunting and fishing rights within larger, bounded uplands. By the late 1960s, most of the uplands anywhere near the river had been divided into individually owned lots. Most adult Runa had or had claimed title to one of these plots. Although the system of land tenure changed, the pattern of land use remained relatively unmodified throughout the period.

Though the land had been formally divided and titled, there was no local need for or external demand to intensify or otherwise modify production on the newly acquired lots. Because the primary horticultural space remained communal, there was no local reason to alter land use patterns. Throughout the 1960s, most members of the muntun maintained their principal gardens on the Isla. They used their large, privately owned lots for secondary gardens but did not exploit them intensively. This lack of congruence between the new system of land tenure and the old pattern of land use not only illustrates indigenous economic practices and preferences, but it also reflects national economic trends and political policies of the 1960s.

AGRARIAN REFORM AND COLONIZATION

Colonization, which precipitated the new form of land tenure in Arajuno, was part of Ecuadorian agrarian reform programs initiated in the 1950s. The persistence of indigenous land use patterns indirectly reflects the priorities of those agricultural programs as they developed during the 1960s. Agrarian reform was largely a response to land tenure problems in the Ecuadorian coastal and highland regions. Efforts to alter the land tenure system in these areas determined the timing and form of territorial change in Arajuno.

Colonization is inseparable from agrarian reform, and in Ecuador both are responses to sharp inequalities and great social cleavages. The wide gap that separates the rich from the poor, coexistent with a low level of nonexport agricultural production, has long been a source of concern and discussion in Ecuador and many other parts of Latin America.

The Andean hacienda, by contrast to the lowland plantation, is generally understood as a rural property under a dominating owner, who works dependent labor, employs little capital, and produces for a small-scale market. A large labor force and a low level of production have created an image of the "classic" hacienda as a self-sufficient but inefficient and underproductive estate that does little more than provide its owner with a comfortable and genteel existence. Though scholars have debated the origin and nature of the institutions, the hacienda nonetheless stands as a symbol of inefficient production and inequitable distribution of wealth. As such, it was the target of agrarian reform policies.

Early Agrarian Reform Laws

To disentangle the complex social fabric that intertwines a large, landless, impoverished labor force and numerous, inefficient land holdings controlled by a few families, two alternatives were conceived: to either divest large landowners of their property and distribute it amongst the underproductive labor force, or to encourage that labor force to put unclaimed and unused land into production. Many popular and intellectual sentiments supported redistribution. The sentiments are clearly reflected in Ecuador's early colonization laws, *Ley de Tierras Baldias y Colonizacion* (1936). These laws first introduced colonization as a solution to the problems produced by the highland hacienda system. They were written to promote the movement of landless, unproductive workers onto land that was considered to be unoccupied. By circumventing a challenge to the legitimacy of the hacienda, the weft of the dense social fabric could be thinned while the warp could remain intact.

The *Ley de Tierras Baldias y Colonizacion* did little to alleviate the conditions that provoked demands for agrarian reform. Movement in 1956 toward a more active agrarian reform program followed the publication of the first national agricultural census (in 1954). Census findings revealed one of the most unbalanced distributions of land in Latin America. (In Ecuador .4% of the total agricultural land holdings comprised 45.1% of the cultivated land, and 73.1% of the remaining farms shared only 7.2% of the cultivated land [Ecuador 1964:6]).

As a concession to agrarian reform interests, the Instituto Nacional de Colonizacion was established within the Ministry of Agriculture in 1957. The Instituto was supposed to create and support communities organized as agricultural cooperatives. However, with the exception of one heavily supported pilot program in the littoral region around Santo Domingo de los Colorados, few colonists received sufficient financial aid or technical assistance to develop successful cooperatives. Settlements such as the Colonia Arajuno were cooperatives in name only; internal organization and cooperation was minimal. The principal concern of most members was simply to acquire land.

During the 1950s and early 1960s, groups such as the Colonia Arajuno organized on their own initiative, limped along for several years, and died unnoticed. Ecuador's reaction to a large, landless, and underproductive rural population, which periodically entered into violent conflict with landowners, was by then largely rhetorical. Successive governments did little to organize, implement, or institutionalize active colonization programs.

Agrarian Reform Laws in the 1960s

In Ecuador, as throughout Latin America, the Cuban Revolution stimulated more active agrarian reform movements. Five months after the fall of President Fulgencio Batista, the new Cuban government passed its first agrarian reform law. A second law (in 1963) abolished any land holdings larger than sixty-seven hectares. Reacting to the Cuban situation, the 1961 Organization of American States conference at Punto de Este produced the Alliance for Progress. The Alliance encouraged more efficient and equitable use of arable lands. The United States stressed agrarian reform with promises of financial and technical aid for development. Consequently, legislation aimed at altering patterns of land tenure was promulgated throughout Latin America. The lack of any acceptable Ecuadorian agrarian reform program was one of the reasons offered by the military junta for the removal of President Carlos Julio Arosemena in 1963 (Blankstein and Zuvekas 1973:3). Within a year, the junta drafted and passed the Law of Agrarian Reform and Colonization (*Ley de Reforma Agraria y Colonizacion* [1964]).

The Ecuadorian Institute for Agrarian Reform, IERAC, was established to carry out the program. Following models developed by the Alliance for Progress and recognizing standard concepts of the hacienda as a colonial anachronism, the Ecuadorian agrarian reform laws state that the nation cannot progress without changing the structure of land tenure.

The Introduction stated that the land tenure structure in Ecuador has been in place since the colonial period. With considerable rigidity, it has perpetuated forms of production and patterns of social relations that are total anachronisms today and that stand in opposition to the ideas of a modern state. Its main legacy, the law stated, is to concentrate the largest segment of existing productive resources into the hands of very few landowners.

The drafters, citing the 1954 census, stressed that 1,369 land holdings (0.4% of the total) occupied 45.1% of the land surface. In turn, over 250,000 small or miniscule holdings (73.1% of the total holdings) occupied only 7.2% of the land surface. This constituted about five hectares per small holding (Ecuador 1964:6). As a complement to the agrarian reform law, colonization was emphasized, and the 1936 *Ley de Tierras Baldias y Colonizacion* (Law of Open Lands and Colonization) was added to the agrarian reform laws.

Priorities and Problems of Agrarian Reform in the 1960s

While recognizing that existing large land holdings were both socially unjust and economically underproductive, the 1964 law stressed redistribution over efficiency. As would be expected, landowners were violently opposed to such reform and created long delays in the courts. Redistribution of hacienda lands thus proved to be a difficult and slow process (NACLA 1975:1). Consequently, colonization, which was initially conceived as a minor complement to a larger agrarian reform movement, became the most active form of land distribution. Seventy-five percent of the land distributed by IERAC from 1964 to 1973 went to colonists. By 1970, 11,808 colonist families had titles to 415,802 hectares of land (Martz 1972:173). In Arajuno the change in Runa land tenure patterns reflected the dominant land program of the 1960s.

To complement land distribution with efficient production, by 1970 IERAC claimed to have organized nearly 1,000 agricultural cooperatives with over 25,000 members (Martz 1972:172). But most of the cooperatives were similar to that of Arajuno, simply a means to gain quick title to lands for colonization. During the 1960s, little was done to stimulate intensive agricultural production on cooperatives or large landholdings. Feder (1971:202) writes the following:

> Ecuador's decree of 1964 provided first for expropriation of land unused for three consecutive years, then that of inadequately used land. However, even these areas can be taken out of the land reform program if the owners present "investment plans," presumably for the improvement of the estates. But there is no provision which determines what is to occur if these plans are not carried out, and the decree contains no deadlines with respect to the intensity of land use under the investment plan.

IERAC was partially to blame for this situation. During the 1960s, a nine-person, government-appointed directorate controlled the agency. The majority were large landowners trying to prevent divestiture of their best lands. Although 28,262 families received land through IERAC, the average holding was less than eight hectares, and in many cases these small holdings were the least arable sections of large land holdings (Hurtado and Herudek 1974:100, Martz 1972:173).

The total number of relatively unproductive minifundia actually increased (NACLA 1975:13). Large landlords, in turn, argued that because their land was in precarious tenure, they were unwilling to make the investments necessary to increase production. NACLA (1975:15) noted that "the surplus generated by large agricultural holdings in the highlands was not reinvested to raise productivity but was filtered into urban land speculation, construction, and luxurious consumption." A similar report by the Banco Nacional de Fomento stressed the social tensions created by, on the one hand, the threat of agrarian reform and, on the other, by imbalanced distribution, revealing many of the feelings of cautious landowners (Banco de Fomento, et al. 1974:5).

By the late 1960s, it was clear that the initial goals of simultaneous democratization and intensification were not being realized. Vague legislation, government inaction, and prolonged litigation enabled large landowners to release small sectors of relatively undesirable land and postpone, often for years, litigation concerning their remaining property. Despite such delays, large agriculturalists were usually unwilling to improve their land or their technology in order to increase production.

In fact, *latifundias,* large land holdings, produced less food for domestic consumption than they had during the pre-agrarian reform period. Many landowners argued that bad weather was the cause of low productivity (Banco Nacional de Fomento, et al. 1974:9). However, studies indicated that Ecuador was quite capable of maintaining a considerably higher level of production (NACLA 1975). Regardless, by 1970, overall production continued to decrease. In 1967, basic imports of wheat, barley, rice, corn, and sugar amounted to 370 million sucres. By 1972, they reached 700 million (Banco Nacional de Fomento, et al. 1974:10). Large landowners were simply not producing as much as they could, and IERAC was either incapable or unwilling to force them into more intensive production.

In February 1970, President Velasco Ibarra, hoping to reform IERAC, revoked the organization's autonomous status and incorporated it within the Ministry of Agriculture. He also reformed the directorate such that government appointees made up the majority (Martz 1972:174).

Such changes had little effect, however. Martz (1972:173) noted that by the end of the 1960s

> ...the history of agrarian reform in Ecuador stood as one of effusive public pronouncements but limited accomplishments. It had done little for the vast majority of the rural populace, land tenure practices were not greatly changed, and overall agricultural productivity had not grown significantly.

Impact on Arajuno

During the 1960s, large portions of Runa territory were treated as *tierras baldias,* uncultivated and, by extension, unoccupied state lands. They were therefore considered open for colonization. Large sections of land were divided and apportioned, thereby giving the appearance of an equitable balance between arable land and landowners. However, what appeared to be the process of democratization was actually the development of an "escape valve" through which the pressures created by demands for redistribution of highland haciendas could gradually be released. Meanwhile, wholesale allocation of land did not lead to increased production.

In the first place, IERAC was not actively concerned with the use of newly acquired land and therefore made few demands on new landowners. In the second place, there was little incentive for the Runa to work the newly acquired land. They continued to use the rich and easily cultivated Isla alluvium for most of their horticultural production. Finally, even if the new small landowners wanted to intensify production by expanding cultivation onto their assigned plots, existing credit policies severely limited their possibilities. In the absence of either local or supra-local demands or incentives, the average Runa did not intensify production on their newly acquired properties. In most cases, the land remained idle.

CATTLE, CHANGING NATIONAL POLICIES, PETROLEUM, AND AGRARIAN REFORM LAWS: THE 1970S

From 1973 to 1974, land use patterns in Arajuno changed radically. Landowners cleared extensive portions of their holdings and planted pasture. Following this, over a hundred head of cattle were purchased and gradually herded over a long, narrow trail to Arajuno. Since then, the cattle have multiplied and pastures have expanded. By 1975, all private land in the main settlement had been converted to pasture (except for approximately ten hectares of each lot which was reserved for subsistence swidden plots). In addition, most Runa were beginning to divide up and secure titles for their more distant hunting and fishing territories. Many had already begun to clear part of their land for pasture.

Catholic missionaries, fundamental Protestant missionaries, and colonists all claimed to have inspired and influenced the Runa's shift to market-oriented economic activities. For some Runa this was true. Missionaries not only encouraged their cattle production but also provided them with the capital to start their herds, either in the form of wages or share herding. Their support, however, was limited to a few individuals and did not account for the complete local shift to cattle tending.

As detailed later, cattle management and other attendant chores substantially increased the time dedicated to daily economic activities. They also required a rescheduling of the annual subsistence round. Thus the average workday was longer, and extended hunting, fishing, and turtle egg-gathering trips no longer occurred as frequently.

These changes can be understood by again viewing local change as a response to current national policies. Of these, one of the most significant was a new set of agrarian reform laws promulgated in 1973. The other was a program of abundant and accessible credit. Both were stimulated by large-scale oil exploitation in Ecuador.

Agrarian Reform Laws of 1973

In June 1972, Ecuador began to pump oil over the Andes from rich oil fields near Lago Agrio in the northern Oriente to the Pacific coastal port of Esmeraldas. Ecuador quickly became the continent's second largest producer of petroleum and began to accumulate extensive capital reserves.

This new source of income provoked major changes in agricultural policies that filtered down to Arajuno and radically altered the Runa's land use patterns. In April 1973, less than a year after oil began to flow out of the tropical forest, a recently installed military junta approved a new series of agrarian reform laws (Ecuador, Ministerio de Agricultura y Ganaderia 1974).

Some new legislation was clearly needed. The joint goal of the 1964 legislation—democratization of land tenure plus increased production—was failing. At the same time, non-export agricultural production was unable to satisfy domestic needs. Although the amount of land under cultivation increased by 4.3% from 1964 to 1968, agricultural production did not parallel this growth (Banco de Fomento, et al.

1974:12). Between 1965 and 1973, real per capita agricultural output declined by 14% (Zuvekas 1976:2). The greatest strain on the population occurred as oil profits raised salaries for the urban upper and middle classes while skyrocketing inflation and scarce food supplies plagued the urban and rural poor. Increasing consumption and inflation caused the cost of agricultural imports to rise from 1.9 to 3 million dollars between 1970 and 1973. As oil profits soared, the bulk of the population noticed only inflation.

Consequently, the new laws focused on increased production rather than expropriation and redistribution. To illustrate, the Exposicion de Motivos from the 1964 *Ley de Reforma Agraria y Colonizacion* contained twenty-two pages of effusive, general statements proclaiming the need for equality in land distribution. In the 1973 *Ley de Reforma Agraria,* the second paragraph of a concise one-page introduction simply stated that the goal of agrarian reform was to increase agricultural production and thus improve the standard of living (Ecuador, Ministerio de Agricultura y Ganaderia 1974:5).

Increased agricultural production requires substantial investments for expanding arable land and modernizing labor practices. To encourage such investment, the junta attempted to gain the confidence and support of those large landowners that had previously refused to invest in land where their tenure was precarious. Therefore, the laws regarding expropriation were modified.

Whereas both the 1964 and 1973 agrarian reform laws permitted expropriation of lands that were inefficiently exploited, only the earlier legislation limited the size of individual holdings. NACLA (1975:17) writes that "only two provisions allowed expropriation on grounds other than inefficiency: demographic pressure on the land and monopolization of land through family ties" (see also Ecuador, Ministry de Agricultura y Ganaderia 1974:19). Although both these provisions were invoked in legal struggles, the 1973 legislation was almost entirely aimed toward increasing production. To implement these laws, the government tried to produce a sense of security among landowners. They were told that the only way they would lose their land was to let it lie idle.

The Arajuno Runa quickly learned of the priorities established by the 1973 *Ley de Reforma Agraria.* IERAC officials told the Runa that their land was liable for expropriation if they failed to cultivate or otherwise improve one-half of their holdings within five years. By this time, the Arajuno settlement had grown to a level where the Isla was no longer capable of supporting the entire muntun, and the Runa had begun to cultivate parts of their assigned plots. Subsistence horticulture did not take up one-half of a fifty-hectare plot; ten hectares were adequate for long-term subsistence swidden horticulture. The Runa had to improve an additional thirty hectares in order to guarantee their tenure. IERAC officials recommended that the extra land be converted to pasture for cattle.

Oil and Agricultural Credit

Cattle production requires a large initial capital outlay. Prior to the 1970s, it would have been impossible for all of the Runa to acquire such funds. In the early 1970s, however, they suddenly gained access to new economic means—wages and bank loans.

From the late 1960s to 1973, almost every Arajuno male over eighteen worked for oil companies throughout the Oriente. Long-term workers sometimes accumulated considerable savings. However, out of the total adult male workforce (approximately forty to fifty), only five or six men purchased cattle with their earnings, and none of these purchased all of the animals they owned by 1974. Most of them spent their wages on "luxury" goods such as watches, radios, and bell-bottom pants. Three or four men in Arajuno began to purchase cattle and expand pastures with money they had earned while working for a resident Protestant missionary. Wages, therefore, did not cause the sudden and complete conversion to cattle raising. Again, government policies and programs precipitated the major changes.

Almost all the cattle were purchased through bank loans from the public Banco Nacional de Fomento. Prior to the early 1970s, bank loans to small agriculturists were virtually nonexistent. Loans were available only from private individuals who frequently demanded interest rates in excess of 20%. This situation changed radically from 1973 to 1974. A five-year "Integral Plan for Transformation and Development" (Plan Integral para Transformación y Desarrollo) instituted in 1973 stressed agricultural production and modernization, particularly for the small farmers. To aid in this process, private banks (notoriously hesitant to make credit available to small-scale agriculturists) were obliged to assign 20–25% of their commercial credit to the agricultural sector (Banco Nacional de Fomento, et al. 1974:23).

From 1972 to July 1974, private banks processed 21.1 million dollars in agricultural credit (Banco Nacional de Fomento, et al. 1974:23). Numerous other organizations also increased agricultural loans. However, the most influential institution of this period was the Banco Nacional de Fomento, a public finance bank that had always been the principal, but nonetheless limited, source of agricultural credit. In March 1974, a new program was instituted to aid small farmers. Credit of up to 100% of the proposed investment (i.e., the borrower did not have to put up any of the initial capital) and at a low interest rate of 9% was made available to all adult property owners (at the time institutional credit frequently exceeded 15% or more in Ecuador). Using rapidly accumulating oil profits, the Ecuadorian Central Bank tripled the capital reserves of the Banco de Fomento (from 1,000 to 3,000 million sucres) in 1974 (Banco Nacional de Fomento, et al. 1974:29). The following year, both the volume of credit and the number of loans were the largest in the bank's ten-year history.

Of these loans, 73% went to agriculture. Total agricultural credits doubled from 1972 to 1973, and by September of 1974 it appeared that they would more than double in that year. Credit assigned to pastures and cattle rose 48% in 1973 (from 278.4 million sucres to 412.0 million sucres). Of the total, 78% constituted small loans of less than 50,000 sucres, and an additional 12.9% were between 50,000 and 100,000 sucres. Thus over 90% of the Banco Nacional de Fomento's vastly expanded loans went to small farmers. Moreover, the Banco was able to extend many medium- and long-term loans that permitted small farmers to invest in pastures and breeding cattle from which profits could not be expected for several years.

Thus by 1974, being property owners, the Runa of Arajuno were required to extensively exploit their newly acquired land holdings, were told to raise cattle, and were provided with the economic means to do so. The following chapters will consider the impact of this new mode of production on the pattern of indigenous life and thought described earlier.

Cattle in the Upper Napo

Considerable research, experimentation, and debate is now focused on the environmental impact of converting tropical rainforests to pastures. Although many have demonstrated that carefully managed cattle raising can be sustainable, this venture requires considerable training and technical support. Cattle raisers of the moist tropical rainforest, including those of the Upper Napo, work isolated from research stations and without any technical assistance. Their practices thus continue to outpace research. Most specialists, whatever their opinion on the technical feasibility of cattle raising, agree that the dominant methods are ecologically and economically unsound.

As pastures are hacked out of the existing physical landscape of the Upper Napo, cattle raising has reshaped the area's social and cultural life as well. First, although few Indians obtained land titles during the 1970s, they expected that individuals rather than communities would receive titles more readily. In addition, credit was more often extended to individual property owners. To gain access to both, many Indians began to etch out and lay claim to parcels of land within their communities.

The shift from communal toward private land ownership, whether actual or anticipated, provoked previously unknown sorts of land disputes. In all communities, "community land" rarely connoted random or open access; rights of usufruct included nearly continuous individual or family access to certain plots and hunting trails. However regular such use of communal land and resources, there was a clear distinction between use and ownership. There were also means for debating, if not resolving, land use disputes. As Indians either obtained or anticipated private holdings, no social mechanisms existed to resolve the new disputes. For example, swidden plots had generally been irregular in form and variable in size; suddenly, agricultural land required sharp definition and boundaries. Changes of shape or expansion of plots often resulted in charges of encroachment. Such problems often provoked prolonged conflicts and tensions in many communities.

Similarly, to accommodate cattle—or simply to plan for their arrival—required considerable individual decision making and entrepreneurship (e.g., planning property boundaries, dealing with agrarian reform agents, obtaining credit). Aware that such actions would lead to prolonged disputes, claimants often bypassed traditional authority figures; this not only created conflict but also eliminated a common means to resolve it.

Another common manner of coping with conflict within a community was by temporary or permanent departure. During this time, usufruct lands remained with the community. Privatization, however, allowed individuals to consider leaving and selling land. This threatened the community's physical as well as social continuity.

Likewise, viewed from the outside, privatization reduced the perceived physical parameters of a "community." Borders, which previously were understood to encompass large communal territories, later enclosed only a cluster of private plots for agriculture and animal husbandry. Peripheral areas previously regarded as a group's exclusive hunting and fishing territory were opened to wider access. Most noticeably, unclear inter-community boundaries produced disputes when local hunters charged that outsiders were trespassing on communal lands.

Cattle also complicated subsistence economic activities. They often wandered into and destroyed agricultural plots. Animals that were pastured on converted forestlands—undulating and cut by streams and ravines—required their owners' daily attention. Adding cattle raising to subsistence horticulture thus demanded new work schedules. With both cattle and subsistence plots to tend, total labor allocated to the family lands increased. Consequently, socially cohesive communal labor decreased. Time available for subsistence hunting and fishing also decreased. Because hunting and fishing often require travel far from the local community, adding them to a schedule that included cattle tending was quite difficult and often impossible.

In brief, by the mid-1970s, cattle and pastures indirectly removed several of the threads that formed the fabric of indigenous society in the Napo province; the cloth had not unraveled, but it was becoming difficult to manage. Communities or segments of them tried to adapt as groups, but the emergence of a cattle-based economy made it increasingly difficult. The reactive situation changed, however, when Indian communities began to organize into ethnic federations.

6

Ethnic Federations: From Moral to Political Economy

The Arajuno Runa's initial response to colonization—accepting and adopting new economic and labor patterns and, similarly, passively accepting the colonists' presence—soon shifted as they became part of a broad regional challenge to government programs that promoted or permitted colonization and other changes in land tenure. The new challenges produced the most significant and widespread political changes since the colonial period. They led to a sharp shift in outlook and posture, and with it a heightened and markedly different ethnic identity.

By the mid-1970s, colonists had become a demographically and politically dominant presence within the Ecuadorian Amazonian environment. The change in the Runa's world led to adaptations and transformations in their views and interpretations of that world. This was not some progressive cultural and sociopolitical merge or blend with the larger polity. As illustrated here and as detailed in the final chapters, the Runa maintained many of their shared symbolic patterns of interpreting, understanding, expressing, and creating experience that made up their culture. At the same time, and more publicly and self-consciously, their leadership began to adopt and use symbolic expressions of a new "ethnic" identity as their relations with the non-Indian national society intensified and changed. Juanzhu and other young Runa, like their peers in other indigenous groups of the Amazon region, began to create, develop, and share a new and broader identity—Indian, or *indio*. They thus established or sharply redefined the boundaries that provided the distinct groups with a single, unifying ethnic identity.

The shift was most noticeable through indigenous political actions and others' responses to these actions. However, their sense of social distance and ethnic distinctiveness was not played out solely in the political sphere. Images also appeared within some of the same frames noted earlier—dreams. These expressions, again drawn from the Arajuno case, clearly illustrate the impressions that helped them to strengthen their sense of ethnicity as indigenous people and motivate their political actions.

DREAM SYMBOLISM: WHERE ARE THE WHITE PEOPLE?

Colonists and other non-Indians worked their way into various Runa cultural frames for understanding and creating affective relations in ways quite different from Indians. The Runa developed no musqui or other socially transmitted skills for understanding, mastering, or even asserting themselves to confront government institutions, agencies, bureaucracies, or other junctures of Indian–White relations. The Runa indicated that in such contexts musqui were unnecessary. Whites and their environment were, they said, "always there." Being "always there" extended beyond their physical presence to the sentiments of interaction with them as well. These exchanges were understood to be highly predictable. Runa knew what to expect—the assertion of asymmetric status. Consequently, there is little presumption by the Runa of any form of or anticipation of balanced reciprocity.

The Runa displayed consistent, patterned, and relatively uniform responses to everyday situations involving whites. Skills for dealing with such relative nonambiguity were acquired simply through observation, experience, and other direct contact. The impressions contrasted noticeably with contexts in which the Runa worked and reworked symbols to create models of and for their complex relations with each other. In Runa dreams portraying colonists and Indians, the two groups interacted in a manner quite different than in their dreams involving only the Runa. This symbolic frame for interpreting order, so pervasive and influential to the Runa for understanding and acting, did not extend into Indian–White relationships, or rather, did so in a more muted affective manner.

Their dreams of colonists, as in waking or "real" life, were characterized by few affective ties. A glimpse at that pattern comes from a dream that is detailed at the end of Chapter 10.

In the dream, an Arajuno dreamer called Manduru attempts to make sense of and cope with a dangerous, immediate problem—his son's serious, sudden, and unexplained illness. In the dream, the dreamer details how he manages to escape from an attacking shaman's suldadu and gets his children safely across a cloudy abyss. Then he arrives, for no apparent reason, at a colonist's house. Equally unexplained, his son's chicken suddenly runs into the house. The owner emerges. She is curt and accusing.

"What are you looking for? You're stealing," she says.

Manduru humbly but clearly denies the charge, explains what happened, picks up his chicken, and goes off with his children.

A similar pattern characterized another dream.

My family and I were travelling to the city on a bus. The bus stopped for some reason. All of us just sat there waiting. But then from outside the bus, a friend signaled for me to step down and chat for a moment. [Note: This often happens during frequent delays on buses.] But right after I got off, the bus then took off. [Note: This is likewise a common occurrence.] I was left standing there while my family was carried off so I decided to catch the bus by running overland as the bus slowly made its way up the curving hillside road. As I ran, I came upon a house and lot with a thick glass wall surrounding it. I walked along the outside of the wall without finding any opening through which to pass. Finally I found a hole in the glass.

Immediately, the colonist owner came out of his house and accused me of having broken the glass. I denied this and showed the man that the only broken glass nearby was from a bottle and told him that the hole in the glass wall must have been opened long ago. He refused to accept my argument and insisted that I pay for the damages.

Finally the owner's wife appeared, said that I was right, and persuaded her husband to let me pass through the hole. As I ran to the road, I heard the sound of the bus approaching with my family on board.

Both of these dreams hint at the new pattern of Indian–Non-Indian interaction. First, there was neither sentiment attached to the encounters nor any apparent personal motivation for them. They simply occurred. More importantly, the dreamer did not attempt to comprehend the white man's behavior in terms of its long-range implications. The images were not signs that predicted future events. Colonists were simply, as the Runa mentioned, "always there," and in these cases acting as stumbling blocks or delaying actions in the normal flow of life.

Similarly, the indigenous interpretation did not involve contemplation, or any similar effort, to comprehend the interaction. Nor was there any effort to cope with, resolve, or even consider uncertainty or ambiguity.

The dreamer's response was a quick defensive denial of an unwarranted accusation, an acknowledgement of asymmetry, an effort to avoid punishment, and a desire to get on with other more personal, more important things. By contrast to dreams involving the Runa themselves, the behavior of the colonists did not evoke curiosity or elicit interpretation; it was to be expected. The colonists appeared as caricatures—flat, unemotional, unidimensional, and unambiguous.

The dream portrayal was identical with the way the Runa interacted with colonists. It was as if they wore masks for the white men and saved facial expressiveness and emotional complexity for the Runa. One persona displays distance and little else; the other illustrates a life in which spirit helpers and dream-souls foreshadow the dramas of everyday life and, as such, manifest the uncertainty that pervades existence and thus allow for decisions rather than reactions.

FROM PATRONS TO COLONISTS

Impressions of distance and asymmetry extend far beyond dream imagery. The consequence of agrarian policies—colonists—and the products demanded by an expanding economy—initially cattle, but later oil wells and African Palm plantations—transformed the demographic and physical environment of the Oriente. The Runa recognized that with it Indian–non-Indian ties could no longer be defined by individual accommodation to a patron or an apu (authority).

Colonists and government officials not only introduced new land tenure and economic patterns to communities like Arajuno, but their intrusive, impersonal presence effectively displaced the fluid face-to-face negotiations and transactions that characterized the moral economy of the patron with a new, more rigid and heightened sense of "ethnic" boundaries.

Some of the Runa, including Chuba and other elders, continued to visit patrons, exchanging gold for cloth and a few words as well. But, they said, people like Señora Ester were getting old. She was confined to her home, where she sat like a glass figurine reflecting on the past. Other Indians continued as occasional laborers, paying off old debts on patrons' haciendas. But as cattle replaced agricultural production, labor needs diminished. Others sought new sources of patronage through ties with missionaries in search of converts. But more and more often, impersonal individuals, agencies, and institutions replaced the non-Indians who initiated the face-to-face, multidimensional transactions of the "moral economy" that had linked Runa like Chuba to non-Indians like Señora Ester. Church and government officials (apus), and later the patrons (*patrónes*), had been concerned mainly with the region's inhabitants—either as souls for religious conversion or as sources of labor. But the colonists' singular concern was access to land. Indians and Indian communities were, at best, irrelevant. More often they were obstacles to the colonists' settlement and expansion. They were more interested in displacing Indians than negotiating any form of reciprocal relationship with them.

Government agrarian reform programs and economic development policies directly and indirectly encouraged and supported the colonists. In their wake, they displaced the norms and patterns of reciprocity that previously linked patrons to clients in a web of thin dyadic lines connecting individuals to individuals or to single families. By the 1970s, such ties were limited largely to a few individual relationships, often short-term and fluctuating, with local Evangelical and Catholic missionaries. For the majority, tight personal economic and political alliances diminished or disappeared as local power and influence shifted to impersonal private enterprises, state bureaucracies, and communities of colonists.

In communities such as Arajuno, the progressive shift to private land ownership and cattle raising seemed to indicate a broad indigenous acceptance of the newly imposed order. This could also suggest the progressive absorption, and perhaps the gradual assimilation, of indigenous populations into the non-Indian dominated national amalgam. But though the economic shift toward a market economy was irreversible, a parallel loss of indigenous identity is not immanent. Quite the contrary, the shifts in economics and demographics prompted these indigenous peoples to rethink and to reinterpret the nature of relations, and to then redraw their social map along sharply defined ethnic lines rather than personal, dyadic vectors.

The movement was led by those younger Runa who, like Juanzhu, had left the forest communities to attend secondary school in the small city of Tena. There, and in the larger cities where some moved on to universities, they became convinced that Indian–non-Indian ties should not have been, and certainly should not remain, shaped by individual accommodation to a patron or by the need for passive resistance or acquiescence to the demands of missionaries and government authorities. Increased education brought them exposure to a range of new theories and related explanations for the general political and economic situation of Latin America and the status of indigenous peoples within it.

Progressive clergy introduced "liberation theology," thus linking the life of Christ to that of the poor and, by extension, questioning the church's traditional alliances with dominant elites. These priests—as well as secondary school teachers, university professors, other intellectuals, and labor leaders—exposed the Indians to ideas such as "dependency theory," which presented them with a world system that linked European and U.S. "core" industry, wealth, and power to third world "peripheries" of raw materials, poverty, and powerlessness. Such theories led leaders to question the role of world capital and of the multinational and multilateral corporations and banks that, they agreed, controlled it.

Similar ideas and explanations, initially introduced through secondary schools and universities as well as through informal exposure to new social movements, political parties, and non-governmental organizations, provided an enlarged frame for understanding experience. This led many of the young Runa to redefine their perceptions of the world. They began to interpret transactions in terms of a "political economy"—as broad, widely applicable rules and practices resulting from systems of production and distribution of wealth.

These were not ideas imposed on them by others but rather were provided to them as a tool kit to dissect and reconstruct their understanding of social and economic positions. In doing so, they recognized an ascribed status that they regarded as unacceptable and a set of "property" rights—land, resources, and culture—that were at risk.

Therefore, beginning in the late 1960s and early 1970s, the indigenous Ecuadorian response to non-Indians shifted away from individual negotiations to group positions that were aimed largely at outside politics and economics. Young indigenous people, sometimes aided by outsiders but acting largely on their own, began to restructure political space to better accommodate themselves within the changing physical landscape. They promoted a new sense of boundaries between Indians and non-Indians by organizing themselves and their families into groups. These kin groups took on a heightened sense of ethnic distinctiveness through a movement specifically oriented toward challenging the shape of power in the region.

ETHNIC FEDERATIONS IN THE ECUADORIAN ORIENTE

The first Amazonian ethnic federation was developed among the Shuar (Jivaro) Indians in Ecuador's Southern Oriente. Salesian missionaries and a small number of Shuar leaders there helped to link dispersed households into administrative units called *centros*. In late 1961, reacting to an influx of colonists into the relatively fertile Upano Valley and to the regional agrarian policies that encouraged and supported the colonists, twenty-three Shuar centro leaders and several progressive Salesian missionaries met and formed the *Asociación de Centros "Jivaros"* (Shuar). Within a year, six local associations (*asociaciones*) joined to form the *Federacion de Centros Shuar*, or Shuar Federation, and were accorded formal recognition by the Ministry of Social Welfare in 1964 (CONAIE 1988, Federacion de Centros Shuar 1976, Salazar 1981).

Four years later, the Shuar example spurred similar organizations to form, led by several young Runa teachers from the Tena–Archidona region. These leaders linked six communities to form the *Federacion Provincial de Campesinos del Napo* (FEPOCAN) that, in turn, obtained formal recognition in 1969. Significantly, during FEPOCAN's Third Congress (1973) several member groups expressed concern that they were being absorbed by broad, national political organizations and interests. Stressing the need to maintain a unique indigenous culture, they renamed themselves the Federation of Indian Organizations of Napo, FOIN.

The Upper Napo region was not one of the centers of government-directed colonization such as existed in the Upano Valley of Morona–Santiago, and later in the oil regions of Lago Agrio. However, spontaneous colonization increased—first, when a road connected the city of Puyo with the Napo River in the 1960s and later, in the early 1970s, when a bridge allowed vehicle traffic to flow directly to Tena. In the late 1970s, a second road, this one from the north, directly linked Tena–Archidona with Quito. With these increased avenues of access, the colonist population of Tena grew rapidly. This increased and exacerbated existing disputes over land claims between the area's numerous Indian communities, the Josephine mission, and the colonists already established in the area.

Initially FOIN had the support, albeit cautious, of the local, generally quite conservative Josephine missionaries who provided them with weekly Quichua-language radio broadcast time. But, as Runa leaders explain, "when it became clear that we were not under their tutelage, 'differences arose' and we separated" (CONAIE 1988:48). Thus unlike the Shuar Federation, FOIN did not enjoy either economic or institutional support from the area's missionaries. On the contrary, as FOIN grew more outspoken in terms of land rights, the Josephines and the Fundamental Protestant (Evangelical) missionaries openly and vocally opposed the organization. They were joined by many of the local political leaders and merchants who had dominated the area's economy and enjoyed their position in the region's strong patron–client ties.

FOIN initially undertook a few small and largely unsuccessful efforts to create marketing cooperatives of agricultural goods. However, the organizations focused largely on increasing the number of affiliated communities and creating a common sense of their past and present condition in the face of increased colonization.

AGRARIAN REFORM AND COLONIZATION

As indicated earlier, throughout the Amazon region, the most noticeable consequence of national agrarian reform in

Ecuador was lowland Amazonian colonization. Though the Indians of Arajuno initially responded by successfully seeking individual family land titles, many other communities sought community land titles as *comunas*, or Indian communities through the separate *Ley de Comunidades Indigenas*. However, the national agrarian reform agency, IERAC, was notoriously slow to provide such titles to Indians, either as communities or as individuals, particularly in highly desirable areas such as the Upper Napo province and Shuar's rich Upano Valley. IERAC, and later (in 1978) the National Institute for the Colonization of the Ecuadorian Amazon (INCRAE), became subjects of regular attacks at annual FOIN Congresses. In this way, FOIN and the numerous indigenous organizations that followed their example shifted the focus away from individual ties and worked to establish their place within the larger national society.

Their actions reflected a significant shift in their sense of place in society. During the first part of nearly every meeting or assembly, and in local training and recruitment sessions within communities, the organizations' leaders emphasize that they first focus on "an analysis of the problems and indigenous perspective" before moving toward any resolutions, programs, or administrative work (CONAIE 1989:111). This formal critical analysis reflects their move away from accepting dependency toward locating themselves within a broader social and political landscape.

Such concerns led to a quantum leap in local organization and a shift in posture. At an August 1980 meeting in the small Amazonian city of Puyo, representatives from five of the newly formed ethnic federations of the Amazon region, as well as numerous invited national and international guests, met for three days. The major concern, again, was the threat posed by colonization and its implementing agency, IERAC. However, rather than continue requesting titles to community lands, the representatives first called for eliminating the colonization section from the Law of Agrarian Reform, then shifted their demands toward government recognition of traditional land rights and for the return of lands taken by the missions from indigenous communities. This represented a notable shift in position from individual, state-granted titles toward simple, broad recognition of traditional occupations. If successful, the demands would raise the Indians to a higher level of parity. At the same time, and perhaps more significantly, the individual communities and broader regional federations joined to form the Confederation of Indigenous Nations of the Ecuadorian Amazon (CONFENIAE) to promote these issues.

Two months later, in October 1980, the leaders of CONFE-NIAE met in another Amazonian city, Sucua, with several leaders of one of the larger Andean Indian organizations, ECUARUNARI. They agreed to form a Coordinating Commission to define and create a future national level organization, which they named the *Consejo de Coordinación de las Nacionalidades Indígenas del Ecuador* (CONACNIE). By the time its congress convened in 1982, CONFENIAE was actively recruiting the region's smaller groups—Cofan, Siona–Secoya and Huaorani—and supporting their land claims.

Four years later, in November 1986, 500 delegates from twenty-seven organizations met to move beyond simple coordination at the national level to form a clearly unified national movement, the *Confederación de Nacionalidades Indígenas del Ecuador* (CONAIE). They thus formally linked the Amazon region with groups from the highlands and coast, and they followed the same general principles regarding land, respect for culture, and representation within a pluricultural nation.

In the Amazonian region, there were also strong statements to the effect that CONFENIAE would undertake such specific projects as regional bilingual education. As such, they called for an end to the agreement between the Ministry of Education and the Catholic University's bilingual education program. Their main criticism was not with the education project's content but with the fact that CONFENIAE was not formally recognized or included in the process.

By the early 1980s, the two largest populations of Ecuadorian Amazonian Indians, the Quichua (Runa) and the Shuar, had organized their previously disparate communities into ethnic federations; these in turn united to form regional and national level organizations. Subsequently, other smaller groups gradually organized and incorporated themselves into the structure. To a greater extent than in any other Latin American country, the Ecuadorian Indians' response to colonization and other external threats to their land and resources was to mobilize a new national political sector revolving around a shared ethnic identity—indio.

ETHNIC FEDERATIONS

Ethnic federations, though initiated in the Ecuadorian Amazon, have now established themselves throughout the Amazon basin. At present, Ecuador, Colombia, Peru, and Bolivia contain the largest and most active organizations. Moreover, these communities have organized into local and regional ethnic federations, national pan-tribal units, and, most recently, international organizations (*Cultural Survival Quarterly* 1984; Smith 1984, 1985).

The federations maintain three primary concerns: (1) to defend their member communities' rights to land and resources, (2) to expand and strengthen their organizations, and (3) to maintain their unique ethnic identity (Smith 1983). In many ways, they resemble other popular organizations. However, their insistence on maintaining their distinct cultural identity differentiates them from labor unions and similar social movements in other parts of Latin America.

7

Ethnic Federations and Government Policies: Indigenous Priorities

RETHINKING STEREOTYPES

Despite the impressive organizational work of young leaders like Juanzhu, for a variety of reasons their actions are often misunderstood. Some images are blurred by outsiders who rather romantically promote Amazonian indigenous peoples as the "ultimate resource managers" and thus the logical "stewards" of fragile ecosystems. Other casual observers and interest groups suggest that the current indigenous Amazonian situation is one of tragic retreat, a loss of "culture," or even an extinction caused by an expanding frontier opened by colonists and extractive industries such as timber, oil, and mining. Others have become somewhat cynical viewers who point to some indigenous people's resource depredation or cite their failed resource management "projects" as typical of contemporary Amazonian Indians, particularly the leaders, who seem to have forgotten or neglected the wise resource use practiced by elders such as Chuba.

Indeed, some of the newly formed indigenous federations' political actions and their related entry into "community development" projects appear to outsiders as erratic traverses between short-term opportunities, crises, and failures. They are explained in terms of inexperience, immaturity, lack of direction, or caprice. Glimpses of specific cases or individual behaviors in the current, recently-democratic Latin American political arena often support these critical positions. Federations, however, are dynamic political movements whose role is to shift populations from passive objects to active subjects. Images formed by outside observers are often moments in time rather than permanent conditions. In many cases, the fluidity of the indigenous movement has not yet allowed these organizations to be transformed into concrete or predictable institutions. Nevertheless, though Juanzhu and his friends have sometimes stumbled over short-term decisions, their responses to perceived opportunities and threats suggest that there is a compass, a course, and a pace—albeit irregular—that illustrates the priorities of the organizations' leadership. The route is the result of choices, decisions, and movements through obstacles and opportunities. That track is often muddied by the micro-politics and individual opportunism that characterize most political activity.

A brief chronological review of FOIN's development from 1980 to 1992 demonstrates how these Runa, like many other indigenous organizations, have prioritized their work. They seek first to alter the political and economic nature of the ethnic boundaries and, thus, the plural societies in which they live. Related activities and priorities also demonstrate to outside observers—negative and positive, romantic and cynical—the Runa's (and by extension, other contemporary indigenous groups') interest in managing their natural resources and their capacity to do so. However, their efforts to advance a political agenda while publicly promoting (or accepting) conservation issues are perhaps best understood as a means to balance responses to: (1) national political opportunities and openings, (2) international alliances, (3) local and global environmental concerns, and (4) donor support for federation-sponsored local development projects.

A recent series of events illustrates how these opportunities combine and manifest themselves. They also suggest the preferred status these indigenous peoples seek with regard to land and resource rights.

1. During the mid-1970s, a North American agronomist designed an integrated land use system for the fragile tropical forest ecosystem of the Ecuadorian Amazon. Combining subsistence agriculture and small animal husbandry, he argued that this model farm would meet a family's subsistence and market economic needs indefinitely, and it would do so on an ecologically sustainable basis.

At a 1978 seminar, the schema was presented to an audience of national agrarian reform officials, land use specialists and representatives of the region's indigenous organizations. It drew nods of approval from most and a few obligatory technical questions from colleagues. The indigenous representatives rejected it summarily.

Indian leaders regarded the project's land-use technology as irrelevant; they opposed the size of the model. It was designed for a 50-hectare plot, the standard holding awarded to colonists by the government agrarian reform agency called the National Institute of Agrarian Reform and Colonization (IERAC). That agency, Indians argued, had encouraged colonists into the Amazon region and had defined appropriate land units without ever taking into consideration traditional indigenous claims or future needs.

2. Four years later, the director of Ecuador's National Forestry Directorate met with three leaders of the same Indian organizations. He invited local indigenous participation in conservation programs encouraged by new forestry legislation. Specifically, the director suggested that Indian organizations collaborate by nominating members to serve as guards within protected forest lands.

The Indian representatives rejected the offer. They left the meeting after politely indicating that their organizations should have taken part in the formal meetings in which IERAC and the National Forestry Directorate determined new land use rules, rather than simply assisting in their subsequent implementation.

3. In 1986, the Executive Director of IERAC serving under President Leon Febres Cordero regularly refused to

meet with representatives of CONFENIAE or any of its affiliates, including FOIN, or to consider their land claims. Meanwhile, the Ministry of Social Welfare formally recognized and inscribed (i.e., gave *personería jurídica* to) several new "Indian organizations," despite clearly substantiated charges that their leaders had embezzled funds from the more established organizations in order to create the new groups. During the same period, while government lending agencies pledged project funds to these new organizations, the existing federations received unprecedented levels of financial support from international nongovernmental agencies (NGOs) for a wide range of development projects.

4. In 1988, a new government led by President Roderigo Borja took office. He selected three close personal advisors to meet every Tuesday from 11:00 A.M. to 1:00 P.M. with representatives of CONAIE, CONFENIAE, and ECUARUNARI to discuss any common concerns. Attendance by these Indian organizations, however, was irregular and unenthusiastic, and the sessions produced no new policy statements or initiatives.

5. Eight months later, in May 1988, indigenous leaders from CONAIE, CONFENIAE, OPIP, and FOIN accompanied four officials—one member of the presidential advisory committee, the executive director of IERAC, a representative of the National Petroleum Corporation (CEPE, now Petroecuador), and a representative of ARCO oil company—to the small jungle Indian village of Sarayacu. They flew in to negotiate resolution of a heated dispute between that community and encroaching oil exploration teams.

Then, supported by over 150 community members, the Indians leaders sequestered the government officials for several days. Amidst constant national press and live radio coverage of what became known as "kidnappings," the Indians and government officials remained in Sarayacu until they finalized a broad agreement, later referred to as the "Sarayacu Accords." It began with an agreement to halt exploratory oil work until land claims were settled. The agreement also included acceptance of a broad set of land claims (including a petition from seven communities affiliated with

FOIN), natural resource rights, bilingual education, and development programs.
Stating that they were pleased to negotiate "for the first time as equals to equals," the leaders of the organizations proudly displayed the agreement. Ironically, most of the items were the sorts of issues that would have made up the agenda for the poorly-attended government meetings.

6. In June 1990, the government's failure to advance on the agreement, as well as on similar land-related issues in the Ecuadorian highlands, was among the expressed motives for a national, nonviolent Indian uprising *(Levantamiento General)* that paralyzed much of the Andean and Amazon region for several days (Macas 1995).

7. In July 1996, the ex-president of CONAIE and one of the architects of the *Levantamiento General,* Luis Macas, was elected as a national-level representative to the Ecuadorian Congress. He was elected along with about seventy other Indian leaders who won elections as representatives, councilmen, and mayors. This represented the largest number of Indians ever elected to public office in Ecuador—a country where, officially and thus minimally, 46% of the population is classified as Indian.

These events and actions illustrate steps toward the broader goals of the Ecuadorian Indian movement. As detailed below, when a particular government administration opened a receptive door, the Runa worked to push for more recognition of their rights and for broad policies to be implemented. When other government regimes closed those doors, the organizations shifted their focus to alternative sources of power or alliances, and they undertook activities that served as fulcrums toward similar ends. Much of the support for indigenous development projects and similar initiatives has come from international donor organizations that promote and/or support "sustainable development," "resource management," and similar environmental innovations. Donors have provided the indigenous organizations with economic assistance, but perhaps more importantly, they have given institutional support, created international forums and, with them, provided the indigenous movement with yet another stamp of legitimacy.

FOIN AND NATURAL FOREST MANAGEMENT

The blending of political agendas and development activities over time was illustrated clearly in 1987, when FOIN undertook a natural forest management project. This project was built from and on the political climate established by the Jaime Roldos/Oswaldo Hurtado administration and has continued through the following two governments. The project took place during a period when FOIN and other organizations were successfully soliciting funds from NGOs and other donor agencies for community-based land use programs. They were thus the beneficiaries of an expanding international and national interest in preserving, or "saving," the Ecuadorian rainforests.

Many "projects" for which FOIN received funds during this period never got under way. Others, such as the one reviewed here, flourished during an initial burst of enthusiasm but later suffered from institutional neglect and disinterest by the federation, despite continuing local enthusiasm. The project history indicates why this occurred and thus highlights several of the broad themes and priorities outlined earlier.

At the same time, the case introduces the Runa's new and potentially confusing view of and approach to their "common pool resources." These include but also go beyond the access and use rights to muntun, or residential community, lands outlined earlier. The evolution of the project thus introduces a new, broad sense of "ethnic" or "national" territories and illustrates a new sense of "community"; with it has come a different approach to community resource rights and management. The case, therefore, requires that observers expand their focus beyond any single "project." Evaluation criteria for appropriate or inappropriate land use must be broadened to include an arena known for long-term political concerns.

Here "property rights," or rather formal recognition of them, serve equally as a basis for discourse over political space and as a factor influencing appropriate use of natural resources. Though unique, the case nonetheless illustrates a pattern common across much of South America—that of indigenous organizations in search of parity. Continuity can be traced through three recent but quite distinct Ecuadorian presidential regimes.

1980–1984: THE JAIME ROLDOS/ OSWALDO HURTADO ADMINISTRATION

Open Doors

During the presidencies of Jaime Roldos and Oswaldo Hurtado (President Jaime Roldos died in a plane crash and was succeeded by his Vice President, Oswaldo Hurtado), relations between Indian organizations and the government became increasingly direct and generally cordial, despite several public expressions of discontent with government institutions and criticism of their policies and practices. The government established the first Office of Indian Affairs (*Oficina de Asuntos Indígenas*) within the Ministry of Social Welfare to provide assistance (including land claims) and support to Indian communities. Though empowered and funded to do very little, the Office was staffed by two social scientists who saw themselves as, and who were seen by indigenous leaders as, general supporters of indigenous issues and as individuals who maintained regular contact with the organizations. These officials also worked with and helped to identify recipients for a Central Bank-funded small loan program, the Fund for Development of the Urban and Rural Marginal Populations (FODERUMA). Established in the late 1970s, FODERUMA provided small grants and low-interest loans to those generally excluded from such funds by larger government and quasi-government agencies (e.g., the Banco de Fomento).

The Indian organizations regarded both agencies as services that aided and strengthened the federations. Though funds were quite limited, FODERUMA did provide a few low-interest loans and other forms of development assistance.

The Office of Indian Affairs worked closely with the organizations and helped many of them obtain essential corporate status (personería jurídica) for new organizations. Equally important, this office had previously helped several communities in the Upper Napo to obtain communal titles to their lands.

Indigenous Response

The support, symbolized by the government's attitude toward indigenous groups, helped to expand the Indian organizations' focus. Previously the federations had survived financially almost exclusively on donations provided by international NGOs and similar donor agencies (e.g., OXFAM, Inter-American Foundation, Cultural Survival). These funds allowed the organizations to shift away from previous patterns of patronage, either government or individual, and to establish themselves as independent agents. As some leaders noted, even though the organizations depended on international funding and enjoyed the autonomy this provided, they were nonetheless distancing and insulating themselves from the political arenas and institutions they were working to enter and to expand.

As the organizations began to work more closely with government institutions and representatives, however small the actual contributions, these ties alone drew them more closely toward national agencies and into national issues (e.g., petitions for land from IERAC or the Ministry of Social Welfare, or requests for teachers and health stations from the ministries of education and health). In addition to the immediate benefits provided by such institutions, these links provided the federations with increased national and local visibility and status.

Taking advantage of the opportunity, the federations directly challenged IERAC's authority. Although land rights had been discussed informally at federation meetings for years and had been the subject of numerous statements, a significant shift occurred during the Roldos/Hurtado government. Indians declared that IERAC should simply recognize and title land based on traditional community boundaries rather than establish its own criteria, such as the standard 50-hectare allocations to colonists. The organizations argued that the government should acknowledge and formalize an existing order rather than divide territory as if it were state property. The indigenous federations thus elevated the debate over land rights and their position within that debate to national prominence. During this period, frustrated by IERAC's slow pace, some Runa communities began to demarcate their own boundaries, thus initiating a controversial process referred to as *auto-linderacion* (self-demarcation).

In what was apparently a partial response to these demands and was certainly one of the Roldos/Hurtado government's most significant symbolic acts, the government formally recognized and awarded territorial land rights to the Huaorani Indians, a small but highly visible population due to their notoriety as isolated and bellicose Indians. In a formal ceremony on April 29, 1983, the President, accompanied by IERAC and INCRAE officials, granted approximately 900 Huaorani Indians 67,000 hectares of land as their communal territory and included an additional 250,000 hectares as a reserve for their exclusive use. Up until that time (i.e., since the beginning of the agrarian reform policies in the 1960s), only about 40% of the land titles adjudicated in the

Meeting of FOIN

Amazonian region had been awarded to the original indigenous occupants, and none had been on such a scale. Equally important was the tone of the President's address. He emphasized that the government was not giving land to the Huaorani, but was formally recognizing claims that had been theirs for centuries. As the organizations had been insisting, the government was simply and officially recognizing existing claims and rights (Uquillas 1984:94).

However, rather than applaud the President's actions, the federations used the event to open doors even further. They argued that the combination of land grant and adjacent reserve of the Huaorani was neither an accurate reflection of that group's rights nor an appropriate guarantee of secure tenure. They argued that the so-called "reserve" still remained in government hands and provided no means for local control over extractive industries. This was particularly crucial, they argued, as oil exploration moved across the reserve lands. Equally, they challenged IERAC's right to determine what were or were not "ancestral" lands.

They could hardly turn around and congratulate IERAC for its work with the Huaorani while Quichua claims remained unattended. The Huaorani thus served as highly visible foils for Quichua claims. By openly challenging IERAC, the more numerous Quichua communities could use the same argument to continue demarcating their own lands.

Similar logic motivated their behavior at the meeting with the director of the National Forestry Directorate mentioned earlier regarding broad land and resource rights. Earlier, in 1981, the Ecuadorian congress had passed a set of forestry laws—the *Ley Forestal y de Conservacion de Areas Naturales y Vida Silvestre.* These laws established forest management as a national priority and encouraged the development of forestry programs, especially among small farmers. More important, the laws declared that protective forests, lands in permanent use for forest resources, and those with established plans for reforestation were exempt from the laws of agrarian reform. Formally at least, this put local forestry and conservation programs on a par with more environmentally questionable activities such as cattle raising. Thus the laws appeared to encourage programs such as community-based forestry.

At the time, however, there was neither interest in nor agreement by the Indian organizations. They were more concerned with how laws were drafted and promulgated than with their specific content. Illustrated by the incident mentioned earlier, they regarded the legislation as another government effort to exercise control over land and resources without consulting with the organizations. Rather than consider ways to benefit from the laws, they challenged the process. In brief, as the organizations jockeyed for space, they shifted their course away from requests for favors, small gains, limited participation, and simple titles toward an expanded playing field. There they framed the debate around broad rights rather than short-term benefits.

1984–1988: LEON FEBRES CORDERO AND "CLOSED DOORS"

Beginning in 1984, President Leon Febres Cordero and a government with significantly different priorities were elected. His administration advocated unrestrained economic activities for the private sector, encouraged colonization in the Amazonian region, and opposed the ethnic federations, particularly their auto-linderacion. The previously helpful, or at worst benign, *Oficina de Asuntos Indígenas* was suddenly elevated to the status of a directorate (*Dirección Nacionál de Poblaciones Indígenas del Ecuador*). It was officially declared to be "the technical–operational agency in charge of defining and applying policy and executing programs and projects for the organization and integrated development of the indigenous populations of Ecuador" (Amanecer Indio 1985:c). Armed with this broad formal mandate, the national directorate quickly moved to assume many of the roles that the ethnic federations had been working to establish for themselves.

To diminish the status of the independent ethnic federations, the Leon government actively encouraged "alternative" organizations. Often made up of only a handful of self-appointed and government-approved Indian "leaders," these new organizations suddenly appeared in many areas and were quickly awarded formal recognition, personeria juridica, by the Ministry of Social Welfare (Amanecer Indio 1985:a).

Likewise, supporting the shift in government policies, FODERUMA began to provide or promise funds to the newly formed organizations. They also offered funds directly to Indian communities, thus circumventing the lines of authority recently established by the federations to coordinate development actions.

FOIN officials reported that many FODERUMA officials remained committed to the previous policies of support and thus quietly informed the leaders that their new role was: (1) to keep the communities from talking about broad land rights issues, (2) to stimulate factionalism, (3) to use selective funding to encourage disputes between individual communities and the organizations that claimed to represent them. One official stated that his superiors had said that they were not concerned with how funds were actually used. Government officials indicated that, though their superiors said that the Indians would probably waste or otherwise abuse the donations, the mere fact of obtaining them from the government could hamper or destroy FOIN's base of support and legitimacy. Given the incipient nature of the organizations and some of their poor managerial skills, tensions between the leadership and some of the communities already existed. In many cases, it was more a matter of exacerbating than creating distance.

However, following FODERUMA's initial offers to buy political loyalty through economic favors to individual communities and "alternative organizations," there was a sharp decline in oil prices and a resultant widespread decrease in government-funded spending programs. FODERUMA, therefore, was unable to fulfill many of its promises. Many of the newly established "alternative" organizations thus withered, and communities awaiting project funds stood disillusioned and frustrated by the government.

IERAC, meanwhile, declared a halt to all communal land titling, yet awarded large land concessions to create and expand African Palm oil production. Some of these plantations expanded onto lands occupied or claimed by Indian communities. Local Indians reported several cases in which they had seen people working on nearby plantations who suddenly moved onto Indian areas, proclaimed themselves to be colonists, and declared squatter's rights. When the Indian communities protested and tried to dislodge the squatters, the "colonists" said they would leave only if they were reimbursed for their investments, or "improvements." Because communities were generally unable to pay such costs, unresolved tenure disputes provided IERAC with a rationale for inaction.

POLITICAL OPPOSITION, COMMUNITY-BASED PROJECTS, AND INCREASED AUTO-LINDERACION

By 1985, the introduction and expansion of African Palm plantations, particularly in the Napo province, and the tactics used to enable their growth provoked widespread outcries from the regional and national Indian organizations (Amanecer Indio 1985:b; CONFENIAE 1985a, 1985b; *Latin American Weekly Report* 1985). The established Indian organizations decried IERAC's actions as government efforts to weaken their power.

Ironically, IERAC's behavior actually but indirectly strengthened the federations. The institution's blatant, highly publicized actions met with strong public rejection and thus served to mobilize and unify the various Indian organizations. Their protests also drew wide support from national and international solidarity organizations and donors.

There were similar responses to the government's blatant efforts to create, formally recognize, and then quickly support "alternative" and competing organizations. Though intended to weaken the grassroots groups, government actions transformed "conspiracy theories" and wild rumors into political reality.

By 1986, the conservative Leon government was reacting to any popular actions or protests as if they were direct and subversive threats to the country. As sharp government statements increased, rumors quickly became reality. Public political actions were quickly and often violently halted by heavily equipped, masked police. They became highly visible on the streets, and stories of police violence regularly appeared in the newspapers.

Consequently, accusations and accounts of human rights violations drew in international organizations such as Americas Watch to a country that had, until then, been one of the few havens in a troubled hemisphere. Such conditions led even the most apolitical NGOs and other groups to remain quiet and maintain low profiles out of fear that the unprecedented levels of government violence might be extended to them.

By contrast, the Indian organizations moved deftly and assertively within this delicate political atmosphere; they continued to hold public meetings and to maintain a relatively high public profile. In fact, through congressional contacts, Indian leaders held two general assemblies in the main salon of the National Congress. Here, outspoken leaders criticized government policies and the space obtained through support by opposition political leaders.

Consequently, the national and international status of Ecuador's Indian organizations soared. They stood out among the few popular organizations that acted in open and direct opposition to the Leon government. By continuing to work and speak out during this period of uncertainty with regard to personal rights and security, the Indian organizations—those who, in fact, openly challenged Leon's status quo—became the period's most active and visible social sector. As part of this movement, they adopted new public symbols of broad indigenous resistance, and they thus drew to them increased national and international visibility, solidarity, and direct support.

8

Indigenous Politics and Conservation

Building on the heightened indigenous profile and facing a government that rejected their demands and refused to meet with them, Amazonian Indian leaders at CONFENIAE's 1986 Congress presented a platform that contained significant shifts in tactics and posture. They promoted two highly visible activities: (1) self-demarcation of community lands (auto-linderacion), and (2) community-based resource management projects. However, as they worked to implement both, organizations such as FOIN demonstrated the difficulties of maintaining broad institutional and political priorities while managing the technology, logistics, and imagery of community-based conservation programs.

COMMUNITY LANDS

Rather than continue to ask IERAC to title indigenous lands, CONFENIAE formally resolved to oppose further colonization and to seek an end to titling lands for colonists as well as for industry. More important, frustrated by IERAC's failure to demarcate and title new lands, the organization agreed to defend their areas by extending incipient community "self-demarcation" (auto-linderacion) to a broad federation priority.

FOREST MANAGEMENT

The activities of the Leon government also led many Runa to rethink their approach to forest resources. Until this time, as illustrated by the shift to cattle raising in Arajuno, the Runa's land tenure concerns focused largely on avoiding displacement by colonists and preventing the loss of subsistence space. Forest resources were rarely threatened and thus were not a concern.

The innovative 1981 forestry laws implemented by the National Forestry Directorate (DINAF) sparked little indigenous interest in activities such as community forestry or other forms of resource management. The attitudes were closely related to political concerns. Most forestry projects would take place under the regulation and control of the National Forestry Directorate, DINAF, which like IERAC was a sector of the Ministry of Agriculture. As relationships between IERAC and the Indian organizations and communities deteriorated or halted, Indians viewed DINAF, its laws, and any land use programs it implemented with increased suspicion. Regardless of any technical or economic value, DINAF programs were, at best, labeled as gifts and trinkets from a government agency that primarily supported the interests of large logging companies and forest concessionaires (Macdonald 1994).

These concerns were reinforced by the Ministry of Agriculture's expressed refusal to meet—let alone negotiate with—Indian organizations. Meanwhile, DINAF, as part of its mandated conservation activities, set aside many forested lands as government "reserves." In some cases, the reserves were situated on lands claimed or held in precarious tenure by Indian communities. Government forest conservation efforts, therefore, were viewed cynically as simply one more effort to alienate indigenous communities.

As a challenge to FODERUMA's and DINAF's activities, the federations declared that any support for "development projects" in the member communities would be reviewed and approved through the federation offices, with funds filtered through the federations. Although the Indian organizations were not in a position to independently undertake the design and implementation of resource use projects, they nonetheless were unwilling to hand over management responsibilities to the government. This stand, combined with the international support garnered through opposition to a relatively repressive regime, helped to launch what some Indian leaders referred to as the "era of the projects."

THE "ERA OF THE PROJECTS": NAPO RUNA AND RESOURCE MANAGEMENT

Previously, the Napo Runa had few options other than passive acceptance of and participation in the conversion of their forest to pasture, as had occurred in Arajuno. The federations, however, provided a mechanism for more active responses to encroaching frontiers. Since their inception, the organizations had emphasized control over land. They received financial support from international solidarity and human rights groups; land was seen as a basic right. However, the attitude of the federations was largely one of reaction to encroachments—from colonists, African Palm plantations, and the oil industry—rather than proactively striving for projects or similar initiatives for the use and management of forest resources.

Until the late 1980s, FOIN's involvement with member communities consisted largely of meetings and assemblies that focused on institution-building at the local and regional levels. But after nearly a decade of organization-building, the communities were beginning to question the exclusive focus on organization, asking "For what?" Likewise, FODERUMA's promises, despite their failure to comply, served to divide communities or exacerbate existing or latent conflicts.

At this time, a new set of opportunities was presented to the federations. There was a growing international concern with environmental degradation and misuse of natural resources in the Amazon. Ecuadorian public awareness of environmental issues also rose sharply during the 1970s and 1980s, pushed by local NGOs, environmental groups, and international agencies.

Ecuador, meanwhile, maintained Latin America's second highest rate of tropical deforestation. This, however, was largely the result of logging in the northwestern lowland Pacific forests where timber could be accessed easily through an extensive and easily expanded network of logging roads, and where logs were easily floated downriver to Pacific coastal ports. By contrast, the Amazonian region was not an area of extensive logging and contained relatively few forest concessionaires. The Amazon region's comparatively limited infrastructure—few primary and secondary roads—made extensive logging difficult. Timber was extracted from the region primarily for domestic use—pulp, construction, and wood products for national production. Even after this timber was felled, it had to be trucked up the Andes mountains rather than shipped downriver to deepwater Amazonian ports. All rivers except the Putumayo flowed into Peru, a hostile neighbor. Any international timber trade had to be trekked up and over the Andes to Pacific ports; even supplies to domestic urban markets had to be carried up narrow slow roads.

Though few federations considered or attempted forest management projects, yet their expressed concern for land resonated well with those concerned with environmental issues such as deforestation and land degradation. Secure tenure regimes, many argued, permitted either continuity of sustainable, indigenous land use systems and/or encouraged investment in and experimentation with new forest management technologies.

The Runa benefited from the sudden but vocal and visible national and international interest in the future of natural resources of rainforests of the Amazon. International organizations began to promote indigenous peoples as premier environmental managers. National and international cries to "Save the Rainforests" were accompanied by a significant increase in international funds available for local "sustainable development" and "forest management" projects.

However, there was little sense at this time, either from the federations or the communities, that the projects would lead to economically sound "alternative land use." Pastures remained the most visible land use system in the Amazonian region. From 1983 to 1985, pasture land in the Napo province increased by 62% (Fundacion Natura and FNP 1988:49). Likewise, credit continued to flow most readily toward cattle and pastures. As with Arajuno, government agencies preferred to lend capital to individual property owners, a policy strongly supported by the Leon administration. Within the Ministry of Agriculture, there were few if any efforts to work with or through ethnic federations.

Consequently, the government's failure once again to consider, let alone grant, community land titles reinforced the image of an administration focused on undermining the Indian organizations while supporting large extractive enterprises. This encouraged the federations to undertake visible, local resource management initiatives. These projects were understood largely as a means to obtain operational funds, demonstrate ties with the communities, and obtain

Project Letimaren: FOIN members gathering land tenure data

allies in the face of a hostile government. In late 1987, amidst an already expanding portfolio of externally-funded projects, FOIN obtained funds to undertake the country's first indigenous natural forest management project.

FOIN's interest in forests received a sudden spur in March 1987, when an earthquake hit the Amazonian region. Landslides swept away a sector of the only road that connected the eastern Napo province with the capital. Within a few weeks, the government cut a new "emergency" road from the town of Loreto to the Hollin River, thus connecting it with the Tena–Archidona region.

By being declared an "emergency" response to provide basic supplies to an isolated area, road construction circumvented standard social and environmental restrictions. Consequently, this road—which was underway slowly for several years and then finished rapidly—was able to penetrate relatively unmodified tropical forest dotted with Indian communities, most of which were members of FOIN. Only nine of the approximately thirty communities within the area held land titles; four others had been demarcated but not titled. The lands of approximately one-half of the communities were suddenly exposed to colonists' invasion.

The National Forestry Directorate then declared all forest lands alongside the road to be under a "reserves and protected areas" status. Though the road was presented as essential, and indeed DINAF did mandate efforts to prevent logging in newly cleared areas, the Runa interpreted the entire project as another move by the government to seize further control of indigenous lands that lay in precarious tenure.

As evidence, they cynically noted that a short while after the quake and despite the destruction of the earlier road, riverine transport flowed normally and was already providing such "basic" needs as beer and Coca-Cola to all downriver towns. Meanwhile, most of the vehicles plying the new road were tanker trucks carrying African Palm oil out of the region to markets in the Andes. The Runa's cynicism with regard to government policies was further fueled as they witnessed other trucks, laden with lumber, moving throughout the region uncontrolled and unfettered by DINAF's restrictions on logging in the area.

Their conclusion was that under the present administration, Indian resource use would be controlled while non-Indians and large-scale industries would be permitted to undertake whatever activity they wanted. Therefore, despite government restrictions, the area's scattered Indian households quickly cleared forest frontage and planted small patches of pasture to demonstrate their presence along the road.

This small demonstration of possession soon escalated to more extensive logging, as individual purchasers and large companies bought up any logs and sawn lumber visible from the roadside and then maneuvered to expand timbering concessions in the communities. Such offers increased many communities' rebuttal of DINAF's control and also sparked internal disputes in several communities as Indians maneuvered against each other to obtain cash from lumber sales. In one case, such disputes led a community to split its territory in two, leading to a prolonged dispute that frustrated local efforts to secure land titles while providing IERAC with a rationale for indecision.

As Runa along the new road sold their timber and signed concessionaire agreements for additional cutting, FOIN's directors recognized that the prices were ridiculously low and that extensive logging threatened these communities' future resource base. Equally important, they were also aware that: (1) a federation-sponsored project as a response would enhance the perceived utility of the federations with the communities, and (2) a resource management project would provide a high profile "environmentally appropriate" symbol through which to confront the Leon government. FOIN thus worked to dissuade Indians from their economically short-sighted decisions. Yet the federation could not simply tell people to give up an income-generating activity; at the very least, they had to present an alternative.

There was every reason for the organization to take advantage of the opportunity to challenge them through a program of resource management. It served an immediate need—indeed a crisis posed by potential colonization. It was also a way to strengthen the organization by pressing for secure community land tenure. Likewise, the project provided an internationally acceptable means to confront a hostile government through selective use of environmental concerns while pursuing a consistent set of social and political goals for the region during a period when these goals were being challenged or thwarted by government policies and actions. However, as reviewed in the next section, such motivation was not sufficient to sustain the federation's attention long enough to institutionalize a long-term technical and administrative program.

Project Letimaren

In March 1988, FOIN began a project titled the "Legalization of Lands and Management of Natural Resources" (*Proyecto Letimaren*). Because the first and main concern was political "sustainability," they focused largely on land tenure and institution building. Without secure tenure, FOIN argued, any development or conservation programs would simply raise the value of the area's resources, draw more outside interest, and thus further jeopardize the communities' already precarious tenure. To strengthen FOIN's role in the eyes of the government and the communities, the organization also assumed a prominent role in the design and initial implementation of the project. FOIN recruited a "technical staff" of ten local Runa with *colegio* (high school) degrees and several with additional agricultural studies training. They originally promoted the team as a permanent technical corps that, though linked directly to the federation, would function uninterrupted by the regular changes in FOIN's directorate.

During March and April 1988, the team gathered data on communities' land tenure. In October 1988, FOIN presented the results, as well as a series of recommended actions, to DINAF. The report stressed that although DINAF was supposed to control logging in the area, its presence was minimal and often contradicted its specified purpose. FOIN also presented the report to the national agrarian reform agency, and they included a formal request for land titles and a halt to additional road construction until land titles were secured.

Project Letimaren: Indian-to-Indian technical assistance

After that, however, FOIN's progress on projects was slowed and complicated by intra-community feuding over borders. Several communities visited IERAC and DINAF carrying contradictory messages. Some wanted government control over deforestation, whereas others asked to have the "protected area" status lifted so that they could undertake logging in the communities. This permitted considerable foot-dragging by IERAC and DINAF. FOIN, in turn, did not follow up on its initial efforts. The organization more actively followed a significant shift in political focus following the 1988 election of a more progressive government led by Rodrigo Borja.

1988–1992: THE RODRIGO BORJA ERA

Expanding Auto-Linderacion from Communities to "Ethnic Territories"

The highly visible, indigenous political actions outlined earlier were part of a large expansion of the movement that got underway following the 1988 election of Rodrigo Borja.

Shortly after he took office, the new president attended a conference for regional heads of state in Caracas, Venezuela. There he publicly proclaimed Ecuador's strong commitment to assuring the preservation of the Amazonian rainforest (referring to it as the "lungs of the earth"). He also described his country as "pluricultural."

The indigenous leadership read the newspaper accounts carefully and with considerable personal interest in this shift of policy. Hoping, on the one hand, to hold the receptive administration true to its proclamations and, on the other hand, to open political doors even further, Amazonian as well as Andean Indian organizations mobilized national and international support for (in their terms) land rights and cultural dignity.

They were able to build momentum from powerful symbolic antecedents. During the latter part of the Leon administration, an Capuchin missionary named Bishop Labaca based in the town of Coca set up temporary residence in the forest on the right bank of the Middle Napo River. His expressed goal was to establish peaceful contact with a segment of relatively isolated and hostile Huaorani Indians whose itinerant movements appeared to be in the path of advancing oil activities. Many assumed that without some such contact, violence would occur between Indians and oil workers.

However, Labaca was later found speared to death by the very people he was attempting to contact and protect. The tragic event convulsed the country. Labaca's death served to release and redirect some of the tensions produced during—and some argued by—the Leon administration. Direct protests were framed by rhetorical questions. Many Ecuadorians openly asked what sort of national political and economic priorities could have permitted such a confrontation of circumstances and actors that produced this tragedy. The indigenous organizations moved into some of the political space opened by these events.

Seizing on this national emotional opportunity and following on the continuing concerns with protecting the Huaorani, CONFENIAE began intensive plans for demarcating their entire "traditional territory." Teams from each of the Huaorani's neighboring Quichua federations—OPIP on the southwest, FOIN on the northwest and FECUNAE on the north—began to physically cut a 600-kilometer perimeter through the forest around Huaorani land. At the same time, particularly in the case of OPIP but also in cases of FOIN and FECUNAE, Indian leaders began to define the borders of their own broad ethnic territory. Using the Huaorani territory as one edge, the organizations established for the first time a unified sense of "ethnic territories" by carving up the remaining area into zones of traditional occupation. In doing so, the federations moved away from a concern with specific community borders to larger ethnically defined units over which they claimed a set of rights.

These claims were a sudden, quantum leap in indigenous relations with the state. Regarding land, it was no longer a matter of demonstrating possession through use. Such efforts and arguments assumed that the state had the right to place conditions on Indian land tenure. By shifting to broader territorial demands, the organizations were working to change the basic rules regarding land in general, not simply its boundaries.

Resource management projects, therefore, no longer carried the same weight. FOIN's leadership, involved with high visibility activities such as the demarcation, also suggested that projects that worked to secure possession through use were no longer a priority. Consequently, they reallocated most time and energy, as well as the general institutional focus, to a much larger arena. This decreased the interest in and attention paid to particular projects such as Letimaren.

At the same time, projects remained a part of the organization's "public portfolio." As a means to legitimize relations with the communities and to maintain the imagery held by international allies, development projects such as natural forest management still carried heavy symbolic weight. They represented the institutional legitimacy, vision, and power that the Leon government had sought to end through support to alternative Indian organizations.

As such, in addition to the revenues accrued by the organizations, federation-run projects were highly coveted. FOIN demanded that Project Letimaren (renamed PUMAREN in

1989) remain under the control of the federation despite an expressed desire by participating communities to manage the project at a community level. However, by focusing primarily on the project's symbolic weight rather than its direct actions, FOIN's interest and concern with the day-to-day functioning and short-term results of the project progressively diminished.

Kuna Technical Assistance

Despite the local institutional apathy, Project PUMAREN's profile increased in terms of international visibility through innovative technical assistance, project staff participation in international forums, published reports and articles, and general word of mouth among many of those concerned with grassroots development projects. Consequently, in early 1989 and amidst CONFENIAE's broad mobilization, FOIN's technical team moved into a second phase—training in conservation and resource management planning.

Staff members of Panama's Kuna Indian Project Pemasky had received extensive training in resource management and project planning at Costa Rica's Centro Agronomico Tropical de Investigacíon y Ensenanza (CATIE). They had also prepared a long-term management plan for much of their extensive tropical rainforest reserve (*comarca*), had established a program for locally-managed "scientific tourism," and were working to have the area designated as a UNESCO Biosphere Reserve. Moreover, as these project activities in Panama drew to a close, the Kuna staff were able and willing, indeed anxious, to share their training with other Indian organizations. As well as being an expression of regional solidarity, the assistance served to publicize and extend their own work and to provide additional employment as indigenous consultants. Following a brief 1988 visit by Ecuadorian Indians to view the Kuna project in Panama, FOIN invited two of Pemasky's indigenous staff members to train the staff of Project PUMAREN.

Though the joint Kuna/Runa team worked together for several months, progress was hampered as project funds received by FOIN were frequently diverted to other priorities.

Essential community outreach was thus irregular and offered little in the form of direct assistance. Consequently, though most of FOIN's member communities were aware that some sort of federation-run project was underway, they were uncertain what it was and thus questioned its utility. In addition to diverting funds, FOIN's leadership rarely visited the staff offices to review progress. This lowered morale among the workers. Many had begun by regarding themselves as the vanguard of indigenous development professionals, but later many came to see their participation in the project largely as a means of paid employment. In sum, the organization's lack of support did not enhance the leadership's image among either the international trainers, the new "technicians," or FOIN's member communities.

The indigenous leadership's regional and national political priorities also affected subsequent phases of the project. For example, the FOIN team and the project's principal donor, Cultural Survival, emphasized that conservation alone was not sufficient to maintain community support under any conditions, and the project thus had to consider and provide communities with a source of income. To shift from pure conservation to local economic development, the project staff and international advisors sought and, in January 1991, received training in commercial natural forest management from members of the Yanesha Forestry Cooperative of Peru's Palcazu Valley.

Indian technicians first traveled from Peru to survey forest lands and determine where natural forest management would be most appropriate. Their surveys indicated that no single community had sufficient community forest to support a community-based forestry enterprise alone. Consequently, three communities joined to establish a coordinating committee with the FOIN team.

Shortly thereafter, these communities asked to undertake the forestry work independent of FOIN. They were anxious to move toward income generation and saw the federation-run "project," particularly its delays, as an impediment. The communities also began to challenge the project's focus on communal property as the site for project activities, a condition promoted by the team and the outside technicians. Consequently, paralleling the "community forestry project" designed by the project team, actual community members began to remap "community" lands into single family-owned plots. FOIN, by contrast, was insistent that the project be managed on "common property" and by the organization. They also required that project funds maintain the team and provide overhead to the organization as well. However, the leadership's direct involvement and interest in the project progressively diminished. Federation attention to the project continued to wane as interest was focused instead on the ongoing surge of political positioning fueled by the Borja administration's open approach to Indian organizations.

Two political actions eventually dominated and symbolized the federations' actions. One was the series of dramatic events leading up the Sarayacu Accords, related earlier. The other was the subsequent *Levantamiento General*, or General Uprising. Both absorbed the time and attention of FOIN's directorate and frequently drew in the technical team as well. Despite this progressive loss of interest in the project by the organization, and increasing cynicism on the part of the communities, PUMAREN nonetheless obtained additional international support. However, with its staff reduced to two by 1995, progress was slow at best.

The evolution of Project PUMAREN illustrates two critical, current features of the indigenous movement—its actual priorities, and its perceived need for alliances to achieve those priorities. The individuals and communities that made up FOIN, like most other Ecuadorian Amazonian Indians and others in Latin America, had rarely if ever participated in the government planning and programs that most affected them and their property. Consequently, when simultaneously provided with opportunities to influence policy and to advance an income-generating forestry project, their primary concern was not the complex management of their land and its resources, but rather with permanent and secure access to those resources.

Because their capital base—land and its resources—stood greater risk of loss than did their understanding of resource management, secure land tenure was awarded more public attention than innovative management. The Indians' environment, in brief, came to be as much political as biological. The ethnic federations were thus a major advance. In addition, as indicated next, their subsequent move toward "territories" illustrated that these land units were understood to be political levers as well as, if not more than, land holdings.

9

The Politics of "Territories"

As FOIN and other Ecuadorian Indian federations shifted their focus toward recognizing extensive indigenous "territories" rather than exclusive titles to individual plots or single-community land holdings, they directly expanded their role in the national political arena. The idea of territories, like the federations themselves, served as a tool for pushing political levers as well as for defining land tenure.

In a "territory," access—understood as passage, residence, zoning, resource appropriation, extractive practices, royalties, or similar social markers of possession—are open to negotiation and thus do not necessarily exclude any form of agreement or limit on activities. On the contrary, the legal mechanisms that follow formal territorial recognition might include: (1) titling private/community lands, (2) granting easements for commercial activity, (3) creating a reserve or protected zone, and/or (4) establishing a cooperative management regime.

These uses and subsequent management privileges are the outcome of negotiations and collective decisions. In many ways, for the Indian organizations, the process of negotiating is as important as the object or outcome of negotiation.

Toward Parity

Recognizing territories is a first step toward broad institutionalization of common property rights and use. Initial negotiation—acceptance of rights—improves the "working relations" between the indigenous federations and the state. FOIN, as with other indigenous organizations, recognizes that acceptable "working relations," unlike patron–client ties, assume a degree of political balance that often, or as yet, does not exist.

This will require considerable change in the current asymmetrical order that governs the Runa's relations with other claimants or potential stakeholders (e.g., the state, colonists, private enterprise, and often environmental organizations). The territorial debates are a means toward more balanced working relationships. They move the political process toward parity.

Indigenous organizations, by raising the level of debate to issues such as territories, express the new levels of sociopolitical analysis outlined earlier. Actions illustrate one more effort to alter the balance of their larger debate with the dominant non-indigenous society. Through this they reconfigure their ethnic boundaries. Land and resource rights, though only partial expressions of increasingly broad demands for self-determination and respect, are currently one of the principle themes in that discourse.

That debate has been, and will continue to be, characterized more by pushing, pulling, positioning, and posturing than by clearly defined resource management plans and/or new economic patterns. Many of the locally run land use projects such as PUMAREN serve largely as expressions and demonstrations of changing local control over land and resources rather than as exercises in its management. The indigenous federation's claims for broad "territories" openly challenge the Ecuadorian state's claims that these are "open lands" and thus state property.

If, by pressing for territories, indigenous organizations are working largely to create or expand space within the national political arena, the indigenous movement may well be moving toward what is now referred to as an "institutional approach" to land and resource rights (Ostrom 1992). An institutional approach reverses much of the normal governing process and begins with the stakeholders and their local knowledge. The various stakeholders create a set of mutually negotiated working relations that are progressively strengthened through interaction, and these are subsequently defined and formalized into policies that are administered through formal rules and governing bodies (Ostrom 1992: 29–57). Likewise, when there are violations of the mutually agreed-upon rules, recourse can be sought through these policies and applied by the governance system. The logic is that those who help reach the agreement will best understand its nuances and complexities and are in a better position to monitor for violations, something that most government agencies or similar superordinate bodies simply cannot do.

This approach, part of the so-called "new institutionalism," has sparked considerable interest among a range of social scientists, particularly economists and political scientists. The proponents argue that social institutions, particularly those established by the actors themselves rather than by material conditions or ideology, account for much of the variance in the collective outcomes flowing from interaction and conflict. By contrast, the so-called "realists" insist that institutional arrangements are fundamentally reflections of the underlying configurations of power/domination and that institutions that focus on critical resources, even if they change, will be influenced, if not dominated by, the underlying configurations of power (Young 1995:37).

From the indigenous perspective, history supports the realists. For groups like the Runa, any dispute begins with and is exacerbated and prolonged by their perceptions of relative weakness concerning their ability to engage authorities and influence negotiation. Yet by working toward a somewhat open-ended negotiating frame (e.g., "territories" with negotiable access and use rights, and space within the political arena), Indians seem to be moving toward an institutional approach. However desirable an institutional approach may appear, it requires a considerable degree of political parity and power to provide any real balance.

The movement in Ecuador indicates quite clearly that the leaders are fully aware of potential contradictions. Although they would benefit from a general institutional structure that permits negotiation, they understand that new institutions alone will not override the existing powers and traditional patterns of domination.

The indigenous organizations, therefore, are seeking to obtain power through a variety of additional, indirect tactics—strategic alliances, skillful use of symbols such as development projects, and marches for land and "dignity"—to create a positive national and international image and to improve their bargaining position with the dominant national society. Nevertheless, regardless of how broad the international support, at a national level these indigenous actions have prompted some strong criticism and suspicion of the indigenous movement. Some government officials and others have labeled the Indians as "separatists" and as "threats to national territorial sovereignty." Although the indigenous organizations have consistently and publicly denied these charges, the combination of their new lexical terms— heterogeneous groups linked under a proscribed, unifying ethnic category of indio, ethnic groups that also call themselves *naciones,* and lands claims framed as *territorios*—has fed into the negative imagery of their detractors. However, the movement's lexicon is better understood through its own use of these symbols and by understanding such terms in light of related actions, rather than through their detractors' imaginings.

In the eyes of precarious and insecure national governments, there is a critical distinction between an "ethnic group" and a "nation," and thus there is even greater reason to question their existence. Self-identifying "nations" are generally understood to differ from ethnic groups in terms of scale and space. In terms of scale, those who claim "nationhood" are generally larger groups with some form of political organization. In terms of space, nations, as compared to ethnic groups that reside within states, are understood to be groups that can claim or exercise some control over territory and who have either obtained or hope to obtain sovereignty over that territory. Nationalist movements can thus be seen to present a considerable threat to existing states and their governments. A nationalist movement can change an ethnic group into a body that is more abstract and politicized and, associated with a territory, can claim independent statehood. Moreover, drawing easily from examples that followed the collapse of the USSR, nationalist initiatives often produce widespread violence. However, this is not a matter of fact but of style, as indicated earlier; the progression of sentiments from community to ethnic group to nation to separate state is not a necessary one. We return and consider such possibilities in Ecuador, in light of the indigenous claims for distinct identities and territorial rights.

INDIO AS ETHNIC MARKER

Since the seventeenth century, the patchwork of distinct Ecuadorian Indian communities—like those throughout the Americas—have shared the status of colonized peoples. Though they occasionally joined in broad unified uprisings, particularly in the seventeenth and eighteenth centuries, protests in the nineteenth and twentieth century were generally limited to isolated community or hacienda resident actions, land seizures, and road blockages.

In the late 1970s, these distinct indigenous groups, particularly the federation representatives, began to identify themselves as and unify under the single ethnic category of indio. Previously this was a pejorative slur used in reference or address almost exclusively by non-Indians. As the term is now used between indigenous peoples, it serves as their shared gloss for "colonized peoples." It displays their self-aware, public acknowledgment of subordination. The appearance and subsequent spread of the indigenous organizations caused these terms to shift from slurs to self-created, salient markers of broad ethnic categories for group identification, interaction, unification, and mobilization.

ETHNIC "NATIONALISM"

By the early 1980s, and as part of this newly reconfigured Ecuadorian Indian "ethnicity," the distinct groups, in addition to their use of the term indio, began to refer to their broader communities as "nations" or "nationalities" (*nacionalidades*). Such self-defined terms not only fueled the attacks of national political critics but, for quite different reasons, fed into debates among anthropologists and historians as well. Some suggested that there was a significant, qualitative difference between those groups who, they argued, simply invented their "nationality" as opposed to those groups that arose from a self-conscious "awakening" of some deep, genuine (i.e., historically verifiable) identity (Gellner 1983, Hobsbawm 1990, Hobsbawm and Ranger 1983).

However, for both political and theoretical reasons, the term "nation" is better understood in the same way as their emerging ethnic categories. In both cases, indio and nacion are social constructs—that is, purposely created by people to distinguish and include different groups. Indians, in this way, determine who is and who is not a member of the group and also what defines the features of membership.

This creative unifying process illustrates what Anderson (1992) has called "imagined communities." Such entities, he states, are not "fictitious" or "unreal" but are rather reconfigured expressions of civil society, created and formed through interaction and in response to particular historical and political needs and circumstances. Understood in this way, Anderson argues, all communities are imagined and "are not to be distinguished by their falseness/genuineness, but by the *style* in which they are imagined" (Anderson 1992).

That "style"—the dynamic, creative ways in which the Ecuadorian groups have worked to redefine civil society and its parameters, and to thus alter interaction with other sectors of Ecuadorian society—suggests that the unifying symbols have served largely to heighten the indigenous profile within the country and to expand that country's political arena, rather than threaten national sovereignty through separatism. The organizations have moved from a historical situation marked by simple, straightforward conquest and domination to one in which ethnicity has now emerged as a unifying symbolic means to engage the national society.

·The Indian organizations have used their new perceptions of self and their symbols of ethnicity as tools to unify heterogeneous populations, maximize national political opportunities, and obtain broad international funding and moral support. These recent "imagined communities" are working to reconfigure the political and economic landscape rather than to threaten or destroy it. The institutions and boundaries have progressively framed and reframed the indigenous focus, increased its national profile, elicited broad regional and international solidarity, opened new doors, and increased its space in the political arena.

Thus despite (or perhaps as a result of) heightened ethnic identity and sharpened ethnic boundaries, the movement's symbolism and related political actions have decreased well-founded, genuine historic tensions by positioning the Indians at a higher level of parity with Ecuador's other social sectors. This is illustrated by what the movement has done and, equally, by what it has not done.

COLLECTIVE ACTION AND SOCIAL MOVEMENTS

Historically, Ecuador has been littered with incidents of violent collective action in response to colonists', missionaries', and others' efforts to dominate populations and/or appropriate land and resources (Moreno 1978). One could argue likewise for the recent, highly-publicized strikes and marches (see CONAIE May–June 1990). However, Tarrow (1994:9) makes a useful analytical distinction between collective action and social movements; he writes that "collective action occurs all the time. Movements [must, however,] coordinate unorganized, autonomous, and dispersed populations into common and sustained action. They solve this problem by responding to political opportunities through the use of known, modular forms of collective action, by mobilizing people within social networks, and through shared cultural understandings."

The disparate Ecuadorian indigenous peoples have transformed violent conflicts and isolated collective actions into a sustained, nonviolent social movement through a unified "indigenous" identity that both spans and links specific cultures. In addition, the Ecuadorian indigenous movement's approach has, thus far, been able to hold in check two major threats to their sustained nonviolent initiatives—"ethnic entrepreneurs" and drug trafficking.

"Ethnic Entrepreneurs"

Individuals now referred to as "ethnic entrepreneurs" frequently invoke powerful cultural symbols to create new ethnic markers. In other parts of the world—most noticeably in present-day Burundi, Rwanda, Bosnia, Chechnya, and other parts of the former USSR—these individuals have been able to inspire hate and mobilize sectors of the population for violence.

Similar individuals and potentially supportive sectors of the society exist within the Ecuadorian indigenous movement. However, the aspirants to ethnic entrepreneurship have thus far been controlled through various checks and balances and public meetings. The communities and the organizations themselves have thus been able to hold such individuals in check or to marginalize them.

Drug Trafficking

The Indian movement is, like the Indians themselves, resource poor. In much of Latin America, drug trafficking is and has been one of the principal means to obtain needed capital for guerrilla groups and similar movements, particularly after superpower support to potential allies dried up at the close of the Cold War. Though individual Indians and some communities have become involved with drug dealers, all indications suggest that the movement as a whole has been able, or perhaps has chosen, to remain free of the trade. There are at least two strong explanations why the Indians have avoided this easily-obtained cash—the desire to avoid government crackdowns while the organizations work to open space for themselves as legitimate sectors of civil society, and the negative impact that drug-related stigmas could produce among the numerous international donor agencies and other allies.

Strategic International Alliances

At present, and for over a decade, most of the indigenous organizations of Ecuador have established relations with and obtained funds for general and program support from numerous U.S. and European donor agencies, indigenous rights groups, and others. This had led many, particularly those with an environmental focus, to assume they have mutual interests and strong ties. Some even suggest an emerging global environmental/human rights movement with indigenous peoples as the symbolic vanguard.

However, the indigenous movement is better understood in terms of short-term, contingent political alliances through which they receive funds, enhance their legitimacy, and obtain essential allies. Their focus remains on the long-term local goals related to acquiring land rights, opening political space for themselves, and assuring the viability of their organizations and cultures.

Seen thus, the movement in Ecuador can be understood in part as an indigenous effort to expand the notion of pluralism. Ecuador is clearly a plural society linked by a central economy and polity. However, the extent of political participation had previously stopped at the boundary of indigenous peoples. Now through their organizations, indigenous people are working to expand political pluralism by including themselves within the political arena. The appeal of increased political pluralism provides significant insights into the long-range goals of the indigenous organizations.

10

Social Change—Ethnicity and Culture

For the Runa, recent political activities have clearly changed how they view life. From their standpoint as a group, and considering their new economic conditions and political status, it would be hard to argue they are not closer to achieving parity with the rest of the national society. With that, they have enhanced their public dignity.

But what has happened to their private, "cultural" lifeways and the symbol systems that framed them? That is, what do recent changes mean *to* the Runa as a distinct group as well as *for* them as a sector of a more complex and interrelated national society? Do they see themselves more as refractions of public symbols and flat images in this new multiethnic world? Or do they still primarily reflect back to each other to create their sense of self and to form meaning in their lives? Alternatively, do such questions simply create a false dichotomy that blurs distinctions between ethnicity and culture, and that somehow winds up freezing or reifying both?

To sense the cultural flavor of changing times, we return to the individual Runa's sense of self and to the symbols that frame personal development as well as other relations—those between individual Runa and their indigenous Runa neighbors and kin. These are the people who, during earlier times, were carefully considered in dreams because they fell on the largest plane of life—the one of everyday needs and concerns. As the previous chapters illustrate, that plane in now much larger; consequently, roles and relationships have changed.

Obviously, considering the range of individuals and their rapidly changing circumstances, no single or broadly definitive summary statement will suffice. There are, however, several revealing narratives and personal accounts of what life is now like to the Runa as well as for them. The first few shown here are drawn from the 1970s, during the time when cattle and colonists were invading their physical and social landscape. The final account took place in 1988, after ethnic federations like FOIN had been clearly established and were regularly engaging the Runa.

"BOYS DON'T NEED THE SACHA PURINA MUSQUI ANY LONGER. WE LEAD A NEW LIFE NOW."

Traditionally, the norms, values, and rules of reciprocity that guided the Runa's social actions were, as we have seen earlier, linked to a symbol system that drew from and supported concepts of social organization, subsistence economics, and settlement patterns. As the Runa adjusted—or sometimes simply tinkered with new patterns of social organization and political space in response to changes in the political economy and their perceptions of it—this produced some epistemological rethinking and reordering on their part. However, setting up a new work schedule and relocating a house are quite different from, and less traumatic than, new ways of understanding one's self and one's neighbors. The musqui would appear to be one clear example.

Musqui Acquisition

Chapter 3 reviewed Runa skills and powers referred to as musqui. Here the significance of the sacha purina musqui was emphasized. Obviously, as the frequency of hunting decreased, so did the opportunities for training boys in hunting. Although this did not eliminate the musqui (boys continued to accompany their fathers or other adult males whenever they went hunting), the frequency of musqui symbolic transfer and the range of elders who participated in such transfers decreased.

Regular contact with a group of elders was essential to the symbolic transfer of powers from elders to youths, for musqui were not transferred during a single ritual or series of public rituals, but rather through a gradual and cumulative process that occurred regularly during the early morning and evening when the Runa were gathered in their multi-family dwellings. As dwellings shifted to become dispersed, single family units, it became logistically difficult to acquire musqui from a wide range of individuals.

Physical distance was not the sole cause for the decrease in musqui transfer. If the sacha purina musqui were still accorded the significance it once had, strategies could have been developed easily to cope with the problems of proximity. Many Runa were simply not as concerned with sacha purina musqui as they once had been. Whereas most late adolescent males had undergone some musqui transfer a decade or so earlier, young boys did not receive such power.

Many skills no longer flowed from generation to generation by symbolic transfer. The Runa still used the term musqui when, for example, they commented on a boy's work capacity. If he was a good worker, they might say that he had his father's musqui. But they generally agreed that the term no longer carried the same powerful meaning that it once held. Likewise, the affective and interactional aspects of musqui transfer had disappeared almost entirely.

Nor were musqui created to meet new tasks. The affective concept underlying the musqui—that personal knowledge flows from interpersonal intimacy—could have been transformed and applied to skills and powers useful in the Runa's contemporary situation. They could have created some form of pasture-clearing musqui, cattle-tending musqui, or perhaps a colonist musqui to facilitate chores such as visits to a bank, the agrarian reform agency, or other national institutions on the changed landscape, but they did not.

Nor, for reasons outlined later, did the Runa indicate that such musqui might eventually develop. Thus it appeared that this first stage of one's personal development, which also established the affective tone and interaction pattern for all subsequent development, had ended.

Runa Understanding: Public and Private

In their efforts to create meaning from experience, the Runa, like many participants of rapid social change, have sometimes forgotten how history works. Assuming that a social reformation is either underway or imminent, some have lamented the loss of what they claimed were their "traditions." For example, with increased work schedules, few Runa have had the time to carefully weave the ceiling of slender palm fronds that lay below the roof thatch and provided the residents with daily aesthetic delight.

Other have simply dismissed such things as the "old ways." One young man, for example, publicly chided his mother for having sung traditional Runa songs. One would quickly conclude from such public statements that, for the Runa, all that had been was over, and all that would be was to be created anew. This was how some of them talked.

Other posturing has been more urbane. Some have noted that, with the rise of the federations, the leaders have increased their public display of face paint, feather headdresses, and similar adornments. However, they added that it has largely been to elicit public support or sympathy.

In some ways they have been right. A process of change has been underway that has, on the one hand, clearly tested the fabric of their lives and, on the other hand, encouraged the public display of ethnic diacritica. Even more revealing, although some have assumed that their "culture" had either been truncated or folklorized, these public generalizations are belied by other, more private reflections and quiet discourse during this period of rapid change. This has clearly been reflected in the symbolism surrounding hunting, shamanism, and critical social relations.

RUNA IN THE FOREST

Not only do the Runa now travel less frequently to the forest, but when they do go, they are less successful. First, they complain that there are fewer animals and birds in the forest. By this they refer mainly to tapirs, peccaries, and large birds and monkeys. As late as the 1960s, herds of white-lipped peccaries would occasionally feed in a nearby palm swamp on the right bank of the Arajuno River. Ten years later, all of the area surrounding the swamp had been converted into pasture; peccary had not visited the swamp for years. Thus, greater population concentration and rapid conversion of forest into pasture drove these species farther into the interior forest.

Similarly, large monkeys such as the woolly monkey, whose environment requires a nearly continuous forest canopy, are no longer killed near Arajuno. Only small solitary species of monkey are killed near the settlement. Game is relatively abundant only in the purina llacta. But even there, increased population and developing pastures require that the Runa walk several hours into the forest before entering areas where larger game might be encountered.

Apart from the general decrease in animals, there have been several instances in which men have been unable to kill readily available game. One man told of a day when he walked, gun in hand, toward his house and spotted a paca. He ran after the animal, and when he was nearly on top of it he fired three shots. Each bullet simply sunk into the ground.

Similarly, during a hunting trip in 1974, a group encountered a troop of woolly monkeys deep in the forest. Woolly monkeys, when fired upon, do not scatter or flee. They remain immobile in the tree tops, making them easy targets. But the four men, each considered to be among the best shots in the village, were unsuccessful. One shot six times, another shot ten times, another fired over a dozen rounds, and the fourth fired twenty rounds. They exhausted all of their ammunition but did not kill a single immobile and readily visible monkey.

Later the same year, after four days of relatively good hunting near a purina llacta, one of the men was suddenly unable to kill anything—including a white collared peccary and several large birds that appeared at point-blank range. Such unsuccessful hunting, even when preceded by several days of relatively abundant kills, precipitates considerable anxiety and introspection.

The Runa, of course, are fully aware that the environment is changing. They also know that, since they hunt less frequently, they do not practice as often. Denuded forest land and increased working hours are understood to be part of the problem. But in general, to comprehend their hunting problems, they funnel their impressions into the same frame that helped to organize such experiences prior to the recent social and economic changes.

To explain the general decrease in fish and game, all Runa grudgingly mention that powerful shamans, in order to insure themselves of adequate game, convinced their forest and water spirits to lock all the animals into their hill or swamp llacta. For example, when the fish began to diminish in the Arajuno River during the 1950s, the founding shaman of Arajuno, Quilluma, claimed that he had locked them into a pool on the distant Pano River. The amarum who dominated this pool was one of Quilluma's supai friends who had the power and influence to control the fish. In the mid-1970s, years after Quilluma's death, the Arajuno Runa asked Quilluma's son, himself a shinzhi yachaj, to bring back the fish. The yachaj said that he had tried and had been unsuccessful.

Later, the same shaman became upset with others' excessive hunting in his purina llacta. He said that he would ask one of his supai huarmi, Adela, to gather up and enclose all of her animals in her supai llacta inside nearby Huamaj Urcu.

Shamanism is also used to explain occasional periods of unfortunate hunting. After the four men mentioned previously were unable to kill any of the highly visible monkeys, they discussed this extraordinary situation at great length. They eventually agreed that although they had been hunting near the Nushiño River, which was an area that had been recognized as purina llacta territory of the Arajuno muntun for over twenty-five years, someone was interfering with their hunting.

They had used a trail, sacha purina pistu, that had been cut long ago by another member of the muntun, but that man no longer visited the Nushiño area and therefore would have no interest in possible territorial violations. However, other people who resided near the Nushiño had commented that the four excellent hunters had been killing too many monkeys. Among the complainers was a family—an old man, his wife, and widowed daughter-in-law who had settled permanently on the Nushiño after having been evicted from a hacienda near Archidona. They had no relatives within the Arajuno muntun. There were also frequent rumors that the old man was a shaman. He denied the rumors and also added that he had no desire to establish claim and authority on the Nushiño by gaining intimacy with the local supai.

The Arajuno Runa were not convinced, however, and these suspicions were increased by the man's wife's behavior. At a wedding in Arajuno, the woman got very drunk and sang songs in which she described herself as an *auca llacta huarmi* (i.e., one living in a dangerous, threatened area) and a *rayu yacu huarmi* (one who lives near a river infested with stingrays). In each persona, she portrayed herself as a strong and unfearing woman who lived permanently in an area from which the Arajuno Runa fled whenever they perceived a threat of Huaorani (Auca) attack. By singing in such a manner and because she was the only permanent resident, she was understood to be laying claim to the Nushiño area.

Her arrogant and possessive attitude infuriated those who had long-time but irregular residence along the river. The four men were certain that her husband harbored similar aspirations. They decided that the old man was indeed a shaman and was attempting to gain control of the animals in the area. They were thus certain that he used his power to thwart their hunting.

Arundu, the other man mentioned earlier, offered the following explanation for his sudden inability to kill a paca at point-blank range. Although he was a close friend of the focal shaman of Arajuno (he was one of the few who attended *plaza mingas* regularly, and maintained a house and garden plots on the shaman's Oglan purina llacta), the focal shaman was angry with Arundu. He had become friends with a family of Shuar (Jivaroan) Indians who had recently moved onto unclaimed territory near Arajuno. The shaman believed that the Shuar were plotting to kill him and was angered by his friend's intimacy with the Shuar. The shaman's anger erupted in a violent outburst at the wedding of Arundu's daughter. After that event, the men did not visit or speak with one another. Arundu said that following the wedding, his shooting skill disappeared. He had a dream in which the shaman appeared. The shaman was angry and threw cases of Coca-Cola (which are seen only during weddings) at Arundu. Arundu interpreted this as a direct personal attack capable of destroying his aim.

Similar interpretations have been applied to successful hunting. One regular hunter complained that his hunting powers had been diminishing. In early July 1975, he had a dream in which spirit women actively seduced him. Two weeks later, he travelled to his sacha purina llacta and hunted very successfully.

Each of the men who experienced and interpreted these events was the owner of ten to fifteen head of cattle. They were therefore deeply involved in the social and economic changes outlined earlier. Their interpretations of either successful or unsuccessful hunting drew on concepts of causality that served to order their experiences during an earlier period, when a different social and economic order predominated.

RUNA WORLDVIEW RECONSIDERED

Initially, beliefs that linked knowledge and skills to affective relations, based on interaction and projected onto all relationships, served to organize much of the imagery of experience. By mid-1970, it was clear that all experience was not funnelled into this paradigm. Only the experiences arising from certain contexts were interpretable within this scheme. Illness and shamanic curing continued to use a set of logical principles that were understood as metaphoric predications of common, interaction-based, sign–image complexes onto unordered imagery and experience.

In the interpretation of illness and shamanic curing, enemies caused illness, friends and relatives requested retribution, and spirit helpers and the souls of Runa friends and relatives aided in the curing process. In other words, affective relationships caused illness and aided cures. Although shamanism is not disappearing from Runa life, to trace continuity of a conceptual paradigm solely within this symbolic frame does not necessarily demonstrate the frame's utility in ordering contemporary social and economic situations and sentiments.

However, by focusing on a broader range of contexts that requiring the ordering of everyday experience and universal problems, there is obvious continuity of an image-organizing affective paradigm among the Runa. This is best illustrated, again, through dreams and dream interpretations from Arajuno.

One dream occurred in the early 1970s while the dreamer, Manduru, was temporarily paralyzed by a pain in his lower back. The pain was so severe that he had to lie in bed for several days. One morning, while Manduru lay alone in the house, he fell into a restless sleep. Then he saw two men descend a nearby hill and follow the trail to the clearing where Manduru lay. For a moment, they stood at the edge of the clearing. Then they approached the house and stopped beside the thatched roof, peering into the shelter. Manduru asked them if they had the power to cure illness and, if so, whether they would help him. They told Manduru that they could perform cures, but then they said that because Manduru was "reading the Bible" (he was beginning to follow Evangelical Protestantism), they would be unable to cure him. The two men then turned and walked off into the forest.

Manduru said that such dreams, when compared to his earlier dreams, indicated that he was no longer a strong and powerful man. He said that his dream-souls were not as aggressive as they had been and they were not able to influence his destiny. He mentioned that when he was undergoing shamanic training earlier, his dream power helped to protect him during such threatening dreams.

He compared this dream to others that had occurred ten years earlier. In one of these, he and his sister escaped an

The "modern" wedding

attack of supai soldiers by flying away in a special chair that he owned. After recounting the flying-chair dream, he said somewhat nostalgically that the chair no longer appeared in his dreams. As a result, he frequently found himself pursued by spirit soldiers who actually captured and killed him.

However, the sad nostalgic reflection he conjured up contradicted dreams that had occurred to him much more recently. Of the many he recounted, one was a particularly significant dream that occurred in September 1975. Included here is the entire account, as well as some of my subsequent questions and his answers, as well as some critical information concerning Manduru's personal situation at the time.

When the dream occurred, Manduru was under intense stress. IERAC was measuring and assigning lots on the Nushiño River where, years before, Manduru had established and maintained his purina llacta. At the time of the measuring, several of his neighbors were openly critical and angered by Manduru's frequent and successful hunting. The neighbors felt that he was monopolizing the animals and birds.

In response, several of Manduru's neighbors attempted to prevent him from receiving a lot on the Nushiño. This led to a dispute that continued for months after Manduru successfully acquired a lot. One day as Manduru was preparing a new chacra on his sacha purina llacta lot, his son, who was staying with relatives in the quiquin llacta, suddenly became violently ill. The boy was taken to a hospital in Shell where he remained in a coma, close to death, for over a week before he regained consciousness and began to recover.

While his son was weak and slowly recuperating, Manduru had the following dream.

The other night I dreamed that I flew to the other side of a large hole in the ground. Billowing out from inside came clouds of smoke. Others were also crossing, and like them I had to grab a short metal rod to fly across the giant hole to the other side. So I grabbed the rod, saying to myself, "Now I'll fly!"

As I was about to take off, a small child came running up to me. I'm not exactly sure who it was, but it was one of my three sons. Anyway, the child appeared and said "Enemies are chasing after me!"

I said to myself, "While I fly around here, my enemies have been scheming. Maybe they put that huge hole there. If I try to fly over it with the stick, my son can't use it to escape them. Also, if I go over to the other side and stay there, the stick would just remain there and my son would be unable to escape. They would catch him just as if he had been abandoned by me. That's probably why the hole is there."

I said to myself, "We should fly away. But when I hold that rod only one of us can get across. Two of us have to fly." Then another child arrived. I couldn't leave him either.

So I said, "I'll try to take one of you in my left hand and the other in my right." But then I realized that the rod was loaded down with only one person. To carry the three of us through the smoke would have been a bit too much. Even if we got through the smoke, we would still have had a long way to go before getting to the other side.

Nevertheless, we were able to take off and travelled heavily loaded through the smoke. It was as dark as night, but I got my two sons across. I didn't leave them.

Question: What happened when you got to the other side?

Answer: There was a village. We walked up to one of the colonist's houses. One of my sons was carrying a chicken. It was his; he had lugged that chicken all the way over from the other side. When we got to the house, I said to the boy with the chicken, "Stand outside!" But then the chicken ran away and went inside the colonist's house.

My son said, "I'm getting out of here."

"No," I said. "Go get the chicken."

While the boy was looking for the chicken, the owner of the house came up to him and said, "What are you looking for? You're stealing the chicken."

I said, "He's not stealing, señora. It's our chicken. It ran away and I sent the boy in after it."

"Well, then, can you recognize yours?" she snapped.

When she said that, I said, "That one over there is ours."

"Well, go and get it then," she said.

"As soon as I catch it, I'll get out of here," I said. And we went to meet their friends and relatives.

Question [referring back to the previous episode]: These people, the ones who were following you, who were they?

Answer: I can't be sure. The boy simply said, "The enemy is chasing after me."

Question: But which enemy? Didn't he say?

Answer: He didn't say.

Question: Who could it have been? Some real enemy?

Answer: I'm still looking for them. I'll find them, no matter what happens. Someday I will find them. I always find them.

Question: Were they sent by some shaman? Some ordinary person? Why did they come? *Answer:* It's hard to tell. It could have been a shaman or some ordinary person who had asked a shaman to help him. It's all the same. I will find him someday. [Long pause....] I'm not really sure about all this. If such a thing had happened to my son in my own house, I probably would have known which enemy had caused his illness. But it could be that he got sick just because he was in someone else's house. Maybe someone wanted to hurt the owner of that house, and my son, simply because he was there, got hit by the illness. That house may have had some problems of its own. So I can't really be sure why my son got sick. But I am still going to keep on trying to find out.

Structurally, the dream is similar to ones he had had fifteen years earlier, in which a material object, by permitting flight, allowed Manduru to resolve a similar concern for his family. The structure and sequence of events is exactly the same: (1) man stands alone, (2) close relatives come running up, (3) they are pursued by enemies, (4) Manduru had a device that permits flight, (5) Manduru carries himself and his relatives to safety, and (6) Manduru encounters friends and relatives at the other end of the journey.

The dream also contradicts Manduru's pessimistic assertion that recently his flying device never appeared, and that his dreams were generally becoming weaker. From the standpoint of Runa concepts of personal strength, the dream is "strong" because Manduru successfully eluded his enemies by using his flying device. Of the two dreams, the most recent one is even stronger than the one that occurred fifteen years earlier. In the earlier dream, one of his sisters was forced to remain behind while Manduru flew away, and she subsequently died. In the more recent dream, he exceeded his previous power by overloading his flying device and successfully carrying both of the children to safety, thereby assuring their long life. The only uncertainty revolved around the unidentified children; Manduru did not know which two of his three sons he had carried to safety so he could not be assured of the son's recovery.

This dream reveals a persistent, culturally specific, indigenous methodology for coping with profound human problems. Manduru had ordered these images and shaped them into an intelligible drama within his mind; he was trying to cope with ambiguity. His spontaneous shift from a description of a dream to a discussion of his son's physical condition indicated that the dream made a critical personal situation intelligible.

The pivotal questions revolved around cause, intent, and responsibility. The dream was not a facile explanation for his situation, nor was it an attempt to quickly resolve uncertainty. Rather, it was a perplexing drama of masks that expressed a concern, an uncertainty, and a desire to comprehend experience. Manduru's culture provided him with a flexible symbolic schema for approaching, probing, and testing ambiguity. Yet it was only a methodology; dreams did not provide him with answers. Although he had strong, well-substantiated suspicions about the cause of illness, he still had to resolve several questions.

The dream did not resolve the ambiguity. Rather, it provided a culturally acceptable forum for the expression and subsequent contemplation of ambiguity. Dreams, as Levi-Strauss (1963) said of animals, are "good to think." Ambiguity was an aspect of almost all Runa dreams they described. Uncertainty surrounded hunting and shamanic curing; they could not be sure of the cause or outcome of interaction because numerous, often conflicting, possibilities existed. But there was always an effort to organize these feelings of uncertainty.

When approached from such a subjective standpoint, the paradigm of affective interactions was used as a frame to order experience and was consistently used to interpret ambiguous interpersonal situations. The paradigm that was consistently used to interpret hunting success did not wither as the forest receded. Earlier, even when hunting played a more regular economic role, the uncertainties that surrounded it were overshadowed in both frequency and intensity by the uncertainties arising from interpersonal relations. Regardless of changes in social and economic life, interpersonal relations have continued to generate problems and uncertainty. More important, the individual paradigm has persisted and provided the Runa with a basis for metaphorically expressing responses to critical situations. From the standpoint of both structure and function, the epistemology that ordered imagery, and the existential situations that produced the need for that order, have continued. In brief, there has been continuity in the way Runa use symbols to create a personal culture amidst radical shifts in political and economic life.

THE "MODERN" WEDDING

Runa weddings, or bura, unlike the stylized indigenous images now thrust before government officials, speak largely to the Runa. The series of rituals tells them about themselves, over and over again, in several symbolic voices. These rituals also serve as a means to test and exercise social organization. In both senses, one recent Napo Runa wedding illustrated the personal dexterity and social fluidity that complicate any attempt at a single or summary statement of the Runa's situation.

In September 1988, a Tena marriage linked the younger brother of the president of the national Indian federation (CONAIE) with the younger sister of the president of FOIN. Both were Napo Runa and, obviously, deeply immersed in their federation's current political activities.

The couple had arranged to be married by a local priest in the church at Cotundo, residence of the groom's family. For this they had traveled to Quito, where the bride bought a long white, veiled gown and the groom rented a stylish pastel-jacketed tuxedo. In addition, they had been living together for some time. They planned to establish residence in the community where the bride was working, so there was little discussion of post-marital residence. There was also little concern expressed with the muntun politics between the respective ayllu. In fact, because both elder brothers held high positions and were quite visible local and national political figures, they had jointly decided to invite over 500 guests. The two friends also agreed to share the costs and help with logistics.

In brief, the staging of the ritual seemed to break with symbolic and political tradition. Instead, it became a set where two, high-level indigenous leaders, whose daily life kept them almost entirely in urban settings, linked themselves even closer and elevated their status regionally and nationally rather than within the muntun. This they did through a ritual heavy with the symbols of a non-Indian marriage and unencumbered by the sort of muntun dynamics described earlier—or so it appeared.

In fact, the situation was, in many ways, as inwardly focused as any other event. For several weeks prior to the event, as the president of CONAIE worked daily in Quito, his time and attention drifted regularly to the details of his brother's marriage. Discussions occupied hours of the Quito federation's telephone time with phone calls to Tena— requests, suggestions, questions, checking and rechecking details with members of the joint family event.

The president of the national federation, whose father was quite elderly, assumed the role of surrogate father/host for his brother. Likewise, the regional president, who was an orphan, assumed the role of huarmi yaya for his sister. Both were preparing for a lengthy Runa bura that would follow the brief church ceremony. They—individually or through family—delegated *padrinos*, invited guests and took every opportunity to regularly remind all of them well in advance of the actual event. Through their concern for such details, the two not only indicated their awareness of how to host a proper bura, but each took personal responsibility for, as we have seen before, the delicate social balancing act.

The cari parti invited the best local tucador and virisidur and then dispatched a large hunting party (headed by the groom's aged father) to the the headwaters of the Coca river. The family began preparing large quantities of manioc beer a week in advance of the cermony, and the two hosts purchased eighty liters of alcohol and cases of soft drinks.

Several days before the event, the groom's brother left his office, to travel to Tena and there to oversee the final stages of the planning. Once there, he worked full time to prepare for the reception of the huarmi parti. Unsatisfied with the sloping site beside his house designated for the bura feast and dance, he persuaded the Tena Department of Public Works to dispatch one of its two bulldozers that, in about a half day, leveled and cleaned up the site beside his house.

He then recruited as many local drivers as he could find (including the author) and coordinated their actions. He appointed one driver to pick him up directly after the church ceremony and drive quickly to his house, so that he could arrive before the others and position himself to receive the guests who would linger briefly, and purposely, at the church.

When the first guests arrived, the violin and drum music had begun, electrically amplified, in fact, so that all present could hear these two, soft-toned instruments. A host of helpers—cari parti youth, most of whom were active members of the federation—greeted guests warmly and respectfully. They immediately provided each with a seat and some drinks. As the hosts shouted welcomes, they regularly surveyed the situation as it developed and skillfully deployed the helpers. When rain appeared imminent, a large plastic tarp was purchased and placed over the ritual area at the last moment; it not only covered the guests, but it created a setting that resembled a traditional Runa house.

Numerous representatives from other Indian federations (as well as a foreign anthropologist) had been invited. Politely, they were quite properly seated behind the large number of huarmi parti guests. Likewise, they were served after the others. Food and drink were abundant.

The wedding followed the ritual sequence described earlier—feast, dances by both ayllu, the shy arrival of the bride, the ritual marriage dance and subsequent ayllu dances, followed by words of wisdom from elders, all accompanied by the musicians. As usual, once the formal structure of the marriage ritual had ended, the drinking increased, scuffles broke out, and dawn broke to greet the drunken assemblage—some still dancing, others talking, and a few sleeping here and there.

The following day was particularly interesting. Outside guests—such as Indians from other federations who could not be expected to filter the bura's social and ritual nuances through their own local frames—were uniformly impressed. More important, however, was the local Runa response. As mentioned earlier, nearly all weddings generate a few grumblers and, most often, there is close scrutiny and subsequent criticism of the huarmi yaya's behavior. Although there was no shortage of individuals who could have played that role (neither host was above public criticism, for each held high rank), none did. In fact, many commented on how graciously and thoughtfully they had been received. Likewise, they praised the surrogate huarmi yaya. In many ways, he deserved their compliments. He had scrupulously followed the rules for inviting, receiving, and seating his guests. Equally important, he had moved deftly between his administrative responsibilities as coordinator and his social obligation to accept the many reciprocal drinks thrust on him by his guests. The guests noted this behavior and commented favorably on how well he had been able to maintain the appropriate degree of warmth, hospitality, and reciprocity with each guest throughout the event. It was, in short, determined by wide agreement that this was a fine Runa ritual. It had provided them with positive self-reflection and a sense that the social bonds and personal behavior, which they understood helped to define and hold their society together, were alive and well.

Summary

What is now happening to the Runa? Some suggest that—having chosen to enter and actively participate in the broader political and economic arena—the Runa, particularly their leadership, believe they cannot be and are no longer the "Indians" that they once were. Conversely, others argue that with the adoption of new symbols for use in their new political position, they have in fact become "more Indian," this through a heightened self-consciousness that has accompanied their newly-created "imagined community." In other words, they are still "Indians" but are now "different" Indians by being more pan-ethnic and less culturally distinct than their predecessors.

However, the events reviewed here suggest that such broad categorization of the Runa and "either/or" distinctions lead largely to confusion or fruitless debate. To argue that the Runa have somehow lost their "culture" is absurd, as the examples in this text illustrate. Likewise, to explain away that change by suggesting that a new "self" has replaced the previous one is equally wrong.

What is under way is not the change from some ancient or "traditional" society to a newer one, better or less well-adapted (depending on one's preference). There probably never was and certainly will never be a single, time-free Runa conception of "self." What does it tell us? At the obvious level, life for the Runa, as for all others, is a constantly changing series of events. Most ethnography, nearly all would admit, is simply a snapshot—a moment in time—that, at best, can contextualize events over time or through historical research.

Provided that we recognize that we are always looking at some "historical moment" and place that moment within a time frame, anthropology provides the sort of "well-rounded face" for a culture that neither straight narrative history nor synchronic social science can provide. Combined and contextualized, these vignettes illustrate that there is no reason or logic to distinctions about whether an individual or a society is "true," "false," "imaginary," or "disappearing." They are simply, and as usual, changing. To note that a change in conditions leads to a change in a people's actions and the images evoked to deal with those actions, is little more than a truism.

However, there are degrees of change. What is underway in the Upper Amazon represents a significant shift in focus for the indigenous groups, one that not only changes their views but their position in society. That images once so pervasive in their paradigm are no longer incorporated into the Runa's current range of relations illustrates the rapid nature of change and the new social and political institutions being constructed to meet it. Newer images reflect the nature of relations and the individual's ability and means available to influence outcomes. Like the new political structures, they too work to order the Runa's world. In brief, a wider range of images and institutions now serve their similarly expanded range of experience. Images of intimacy and balanced reciprocity are, quite simply, where they should be. They are placed where, from the point of view of the Runa, they can make a difference. Other images and interpretations likewise serve to order the new experiences. What is occurring is not some sort of radical transformation, but rather a logical focusing of the lens to accommodate a new frame.

It is clear that more attention is now being directed toward the inter-ethnic arena. Although symbols are cognitive categories that serve to order all experience, public and private, these order different "sorts" of experience. This obvious distinction is sometimes overlooked by observers.

At certain times and in certain contexts, the more important symbols to an individual Runa are those detailed earlier—ones reflected in ritual and dreams and focused on a sense of intimacy. At other times and in other settings (almost exclusively public), the important symbol to them is "ethnicity"—the social distinctions between groups.

Such distinctions are not exclusive to the Runa. Within any society and at any time, concepts of culture and ethnicity are always present. What changes, or rather, what seems to rise to and fall from the fore, is the significance of strong ethnic distinctions. Long before colonists and Ecuadorian government agencies loomed so large in the Amazon, the Runa clearly had a set of "ethnic" categories and markers through which they distinguished themselves from others. They identified other lowland indigenous peoples through the somewhat generic term *auca*, or outsider. Among these outsiders were the *llusti auca* (the "naked" ones, or contemporary Huaorani), the *puyo auca* (that mix of groups who now form the Canelos Quicha and who are distinguished by dialectical differences, among other things). There were likewise *blancus*, non-Indian Ecuadorians, and *ransia*, non-Hispanic non-Indians.

The prior distinctions and boundaries were clearly and widely understood, and they were marked through such diacritica as appearance, language, dialect, special skills, and other social distinctions. In brief, the Runa have always had neighbors, and thus they have always had a sense of ethnicity. However, until quite recently, these "others" occupied less time and space within the Runa's social and political map. Consequently, ethnic boundaries and related markers were less pronounced.

Since at least the 1960s, ethnicity—or more specifically, the boundaries between Indians and non-Indians—has become increasingly salient in the Runa's daily life. It is thus no surprise that they now pay more attention to the boundaries. At the same time, there is among the Runa, as Turner (1991) notes among the Kayapo, a sharply different presentation of their public self. This is illustrated by such symbols as long hair and increased public adornments such as feather headdresses. Likewise, they have recently begun to speak of themselves in terms of their "culture" and have organized efforts to recreate and display that culture.

However, the settings in which these markers occur are usually those found along the boundaries of ethnicity. They are essential to setting the tone and expressing the desired outcome in any inter-ethnic setting critical to ordering the outcome of political life (e.g., public meetings and international events). These are the settings in which ethnic differences are most salient and obvious. The boundaries that are being displayed are also being negotiated. By presenting a set of symbols—whether drawn from the past, borrowed from neighbors, or simply invented at the moment and suddenly cast as primordial "cultural" expressions—these symbols speak to the "other" but are nonetheless refracting back to the Runa. And so it is with their new, regular insistence on the fact that they have a "culture." Although such expressions may be new, or indeed borrowed from the distinctive categories of the dominant society, they need not be taken literally.

The Runa's focus on their "culture" and their public expressions of it may tell us more about the changing nature of ethnic relations among the Runa than any radical shift in the ways such images—however new—are processed and understood. At that point, the distinction between what life means *for* and *to* the Runa may be unclear. Nonetheless, it remains a useful frame for analysis and serves as a means to appreciate these people as well-rounded selves during times such as the present, when flat images may have provided better political leverage and recruited distant allies.

References

Anderson, Benedict
1983   *Imagined Communities.* London: Verso.

Beghin, Francisco Javier
1963   Informe sobre las condiciones de servidumbre vigente en las haciendas del Oriente ecuatoriano. *Humanitas* 5 (1): 112–128.

Bellew, Frank
1975   Interview. Quito, December 1975.

Blankstein, Charles S. and Clarence Zuvekas
1973   Agrarian reform in Ecuador: An analysis of past efforts in the development of a new approach. *Economic Development and Cultural Change* 22: 73–94.

Bravo, Vicente M.
1920   *Viaje al Oriente: Segunda parte, en la region del Curaray.* Quito: EMG.

Casement, Roger
1912   *Correspondence Reflecting the Treatment of British Colonial Subjects and Native Indians Employed in the Collection of Rubber in the Putumayo Region.* London: Harrison and Sons.

Collier, Richard
1968   *The River that God Forgot: The Story of the Amazon Rubber Boom.* New York: Dutton.

CONAIE
1989   *Las nacionalidades indigenas en el Ecuador.* Quito: Ediciones Tinkui.

CONFENIAE
1985a   *Palma Africana y etnocedio.* Quito: CEDIS–CONFENIAE.
1985b   *Defendemos nuestra tierra! Defendemos nuestra tierra!* Quito:
        CEDEP–CONFENIAIE.

Conklin, Harold
1957   *Hanunoo Agriculture in the Philippines.* FAO Forestry
        Development Paper 12. Rome: Food and Agriculture
        Organization of the United Nations.

Ecuador
1962   *Segundo censo de poblacion y primer censo de vivienda.* Quito:
        Junta Nacional de Planificacion.
1964   *Ley de Reforma Agraria (Decreto Supremo No. 1480).* Quito:
        Tallares Graficos "Minerva."
1974   *Segundo censo agropecuario, resultados provisionales.* Quito:
        Instituto Nacional de Estadistica y Censos.
1974a   *Reforma Agraria: Ley y Reglamento.* Quito: Cencotap.
n.d [1968] *El credito agropecuario en el periodo 1964–1967.* Docu-
        mento No. 08-03-24-X-68.

Eliot, Elizabeth
1957   *Through Gates of Splendor.* New York: Harper and Row.

Feder, Ernst
1971   *The Rape of the Peasantry.* New York: Doubleday.

Firth, Raymond
1973   *Symbols: Public and Private.* Ithaca, NY: Cornell University
        Press.

Galaraza, Jaime
1974   *El festin del petroleo.* Quito: Editorial Universitaria.

Geertz, Clifford
1973   Religion as a cultural system. In: *The Interpretation of Cul-
        tures* by Clifford Geertz. New York: Basic Books.

Gellner, Ernest
1983   *Nations and Nationalism.* Ithaca, NY: Cornell University
        Press.

Hardenberg, W. E.
1912   *The Putumayo: The Devil's Paradise.* London: T. Fisher
        Unwin.

Harner, Michael
1972   *The Jivaro: People of the Sacred Waterfalls.* Garden City, NY:
        Doubleday.

Hobsbawm, Eric
1990   *Nations and Nationalism since 1780*. New York: Cambridge
        University Press.

Holloway, H. L.
1932   East of the Ecuadorian Andes. *The Geographic Journal* 80
        (5): 410–419.

Hurtado, Oswaldo and Joachin Herudek
1974   La organizacion popular en el Ecuador. Quito: Editorial
        "Fray Jodoco Ricke."

Irvine, Dominique
1989   Succession management and resource distribution in an
        Amazonian rainforest. In: *Resource Management in Amazo-
        nia: Indigenous and Folk Strategies*, Darrell A. Posey and
        William Balee, eds. New York: The New York Botanical
        Gardens, Advances in Economic Botany, Vol 7.

Jaramillio Alvarado, Pio
1936   *Tierras del Oriente*. Quito: Imprenta Nacional.

Latin American Weekly Report
1985   African Palm and ethnocide. 8 November. (WR-85-44).

Leach, Edmund
1961   *Pul Eliya: A Village in Ceylon*. New York: Cambridge Uni-
        versity Press.

Macas, Luis
1991   *El levantamiento indigena visto por sus protagonistas*. Quito:
        Instituto Cientifica de Culturas Indigenas.

Macdonald, Theodore
1979   *Process of Change in Amazonian Ecuador: Quijos Quichua
        Indians become Cattlemen*. Ann Arbor, MI: University
        Microfilms.

1980   Indigenous response to an expanding frontier: Quijos
        Quichua economic conversion to cattle raising. In: *Cul-
        tural Transformations and Ethnicty in Modern Ecuador*.
        Norman E. Whitten, Jr., ed. Urbana, IL: University of Illi-
        nois Press.

1983   Territorio indigena en el Ecuador: Un ejemplo de su
        delimitacion. *America Indigena* 43 (3): 555–568.

Moratorio, Blanca
1987   *Rucuyaya Alonso y la historia social y economica del Alto
        Napo: 1850–1950*. Quito: Ediciones Abya Yala.

Moreno, Segundo
1985   *Sublevaciones indigenas en la Audiencia de Quito.* Quito: Ediciones de la Universidad Catolica de Quito.

NACLA
1975   Ecuador: Oil up for grabs. *NACLA's Latin America and Empire Report* 9 (8), November.

Oberem, Udo
1973   *Los Quijos: Historia de al transculturacion de un grupo indigena en el Oriente ecuatoriano (1538–1956).* Madrid: Facultad de Filosofia y Latras, Universidad de Madrid.
1974   Trade and trade goods in the Ecuadorian Montana. In: *Native South America: Ethnology of the Least Known Continent.* Patricia J. Lyon, ed. Boston: Little Brown.

Ostrom, Elinor
1990   *Governing the Commons.* New York: Cambridge University Press.

Posey, Darrell A. and William Balee (eds.)
1989   *Resource Management in Amazonia: Indigenous and Folk Strategies.* New York: The New York Botanical Gardens, Advances in Economic Botany, Vol 7.

Salazar, Ernesto
1981   The Federacion Shuar and the colonization frontier. In: *Cultural Transformations and Ethnicity in Modern Ecuador.* Norman E. Whitten, Jr., ed. Urbana, IL: University of Illinois Press.

Scott, James C.
1985   *Weapons of the Weak.* New Haven, CT: Yale University Press.

Smith, Richard Chase
1984a   Amazonian Indians participate at U. N. *Cultural Survival Quarterly* 8 (4): 6–13.
1984b   Unity within diversity: Peasant unions, ethnic federations and Indianist movements in the Andean Republics. *Cultural Survival Quarterly* 8 (4): 6–13.

Spiller, Maximiliano
1974   *Historia de la mision Josefina del Napo, 1922–1974.* Quito: Artes Graficas.

Tarrow, Sidney
1994   *Power in Movement: Social Movements, Collective Action and Politics.* New York: Cambridge University Press.

Thompson, E. P.
1993   *Customs in Common: Studies in Traditional Popular Culture.*
        New York: The New Press.
Tschopp, H. J.
1953   Oil exploration in the Oriente of Ecuador, 1938–1950. *Bulletin of the American Association of Petroleum Geologists* 37 (10): 2303–2347.
Turner, Terrence
1991   Representing, resisting, rethinking. In: *Colonial Situations.* George Stocking, ed. Madison, WI: University of Wisconsin Press.
Uquillas, Jorge
1983   Indian land rights and natural resource management in the Ecuadorian Amazon. In: *Native Peoples and Economic Development: Six Case Studies from Latin America.* Theodore Macdonald, ed. Cambridge, MA: Cultural Survival Occasional Paper No. 16.
1984   Colonization and spontaneous settlement in the Ecuadorian Amazon. In: *Frontier Expansion in Amazonia.* Marianne Schmink and Charles H. Wood, eds. Gainsville, FL: University of Florida Press.
Wallis, Ethel Emily
1971   *The Dayuma Story: Life under Auca Spears.* Old Tappen, NJ: Spire Books.
1973   *Aucas Downriver: Dayuma's Story Today.* New York: Harper and Row.
Young, Oran
1995   The problem of scaling in human/environment relationships. In: *Local Commons and Global Interdependence.* Robert O. Keohane and Elinor Ostrom, eds. Thousand Islands, CA: Sage Publications.

Index